GOVERNMENT PROCEDURES AND OPERATIONS

PROPOSALS FOR PRESIDENTIAL ELECTION REFORM

NATIONAL POPULAR VOTE AND ELECTORAL COLLEGE OPTIONS

GOVERNMENT PROCEDURES AND OPERATIONS

Additional books in this series can be found on Nova's website under the Series tab.

Additional e-books in this series can be found on Nova's website under the e-book tab.

GOVERNMENT PROCEDURES AND OPERATIONS

PROPOSALS FOR PRESIDENTIAL ELECTION REFORM

NATIONAL POPULAR VOTE AND ELECTORAL COLLEGE OPTIONS

MAUREEN STONE
EDITOR

nova publishers
New York

Library of Congress Cataloging-in-Publication Data

ISBN: 978-1-63482-933-5

Published by Nova Science Publishers, Inc. † New York

CONTENTS

PREFACE

The National Popular Vote (NPV) initiative proposes an agreement among the states, an interstate compact that would effectively achieve direct popular election of the President and Vice President without a constitutional amendment. This book monitors the NPV's progress in the states and identifies and provides an analysis of further developments as warranted. When Americans vote for President and Vice President, they are actually choosing presidential electors, known collectively as the Electoral College. It is these officials who choose the President and Vice President of the United States. The complex elements comprising the Electoral College system are responsible for one of the most important processes of the American political and constitutional system: election of the President and Vice President. A failure to elect, or worse, the choice of a chief executive whose legitimacy might be open to question, could precipitate a profound constitutional crisis that would require prompt, judicious, and well-informed action by Congress. This book discusses the contemporary issues for Congress and how the Electoral College works in contemporary presidential elections.

In: Proposals for Presidential Election Reform ISBN: 978-1-63482-933-5
Editor: Maureen Stone

Chapter 1

THE NATIONAL POPULAR VOTE INITIATIVE: DIRECT ELECTION OF THE PRESIDENT BY INTERSTATE COMPACT*

Thomas H. Neale and Andrew Nolan

SUMMARY

The National Popular Vote (NPV) initiative proposes an agreement among the states, an interstate compact that would effectively achieve direct popular election of the President and Vice President without a constitutional amendment. It relies on the Constitution's grant of authority to the states in Article II, Section 1, to appoint presidential electors "in such Manner as the Legislature thereof may direct.... " Any state that joins the NPV compact pledges to award all its electoral votes to the presidential ticket that wins the most popular votes nationwide, regardless of who wins in that particular state. The number of electoral votes won by the national popular vote winners would depend on the number of electoral votes controlled by NPV member states. The compact would, however, come into effect only if its success has been assured; that is, only if states controlling a majority of electoral votes (270 or more) join the compact. Recent action by the New York legislature to join the compact has generated renewed interest in the NPV initiative.

---

* This is an edited, reformatted and augmented version of a Congressional Research Service publication, No. R43823, dated December 12, 2014.

At the time of this writing, 10 states and the District of Columbia, which jointly control 165 electoral votes, have joined the compact.

The National Popular Vote initiative emerged following the presidential election of 2000, in which one ticket gained an electoral vote majority, winning the presidency, but received fewer popular votes than its opponents. NPV grew out of subsequent discussions among scholars and activists about how to avoid similar outcomes in the future and to achieve direct popular election.

Proponents of NPV assert that it would guarantee the presidential candidates who win the most popular votes nationwide will always win the presidency; that it would end the inequities of the general ticket/winner-take-all system of awarding electoral votes; and that candidates would extend their focus beyond winning the "battleground states," campaigning more widely and devoting greater attention to issues of concern to other parts of the country. They further assert that NPV would accomplish this while avoiding the exacting standards set for the proposal and ratification of constitutional amendments. Opponents argue that NPV would undermine the authority of states under the Constitution and the Founders' intention that presidential elections should be both national and federal contests; that it is an admitted "end run" around the Constitution which would circumvent the amendment process; and that it might actually lead to more disputed presidential elections characterized by politically contentious state recounts.

The NPV has also been debated on constitutional and legal grounds. Some observers maintain that it must be approved by Congress, because it is an interstate compact that would affect key provisions of constitutional presidential election procedures. NPV Inc., the organization managing the initiative's advocacy campaign, responds that congressional approval is not necessary because NPV deals with the appointment of electors, a subject that falls within state constitutional authority, and that the Supreme Court has previously rejected arguments that similar compacts would impair the rights of nonmember states. Other critics claim that NPV might violate the Voting Rights Act by diluting minority voter influence and avoiding the recently invalidated preclearance requirement for election procedures changes in covered jurisdictions. In response, NPV, Inc. has asserted that the compact is "entirely consistent with the goal of the Voting Rights Act."

This report monitors the NPV's progress in the states and will identify and provide analysis of further developments as warranted.

INTRODUCTION[1]

Since its founding in 2006, the National Popular Vote initiative has promoted an agreement among the states, an interstate compact that would effectively establish direct popular election of the President and Vice President without a constitutional amendment, while retaining the structure of the electoral college system.

The United States is unique among "presidential" republics by providing an indirect election to choose its chief executive.[2] The President and Vice President of the United States are selected not by registered voters, but by the electoral college, electors appointed in the states "in such Manner as the Legislature thereof may direct.... " Alexander Hamilton, who was "present at the creation" of the Constitution in 1787, commented favorably on the electoral college system in *The Federalist*:

> The mode of appointment of the Chief Magistrate of the United States is almost the only part of the system, of any consequence, which has escaped without severe censure, or which has received the slightest mark of approbation from its opponents.... I venture somewhat further, and hesitate not to affirm that if the manner of it be not perfect, it is at least excellent. It unites in an eminent degree all the advantages the union of which was to be wished for.[3]

Notwithstanding Hamilton's endorsement, the first proposal to change the electoral college system by constitutional amendment was introduced as early as 1800, and since that time more than 700 proposals to reform or eliminate the college have been introduced in Congress.[4] Reform advocates have long focused on the fact that it does not provide for direct democratic election, and that the winner-take-all system makes it possible for candidates to win an electoral college majority and the presidency, while gaining fewer votes than their principal opponents in the popular election.

Between 1949 and 1979, Congress considered amendments to reform the electoral college, or replace it with direct popular election, in committee and on the floor of both chambers. Proposed amendments must, however, meet the requirements of the Constitution's Article V, which calls for two-thirds approval by both houses of Congress, and ratification by three-fourths of the states;[5] to date, no electoral college reform proposal has met these requirements.

Proponents of the National Popular Vote initiative contend that their plan will achieve direct popular election while circumventing the requirements of

Article V, and will guarantee that the popular vote winners will always be elected President and Vice President.

THE ELECTORAL COLLEGE IN BRIEF[6]

The fundamentals of the electoral college system were established by Article II, Section 1 of the U.S. Constitution, and subsequently revised by the Twelfth Amendment. The Constitution's minimal provisions have been complemented over the past two centuries by a range of federal and state laws, political party procedures, and enduring political traditions, leading to the system as it exists today. The salient features of the contemporary system are detailed below.

The electors are collectively known as the electoral college; although this phrase does not appear in the Constitution, it gained currency in the early days of the republic, and was recognized in federal law in 1845.[7] The electoral college has no continuing existence; its sole purpose is to elect the President and Vice President. Each state is allocated a number of electors equal to the combined total of its U.S. Senate and House of Representatives delegations.[8] The District of Columbia is also allocated three electors.[9] At present, the total is 538, reflecting the combined size of the Senate (100 Members), the House (435 Members) and the District of Columbia electors. Any person may serve as an elector, except Senators and Representatives, or any other person holding an office of "trust or profit" under the United States.[10]

Article II, Section 1 of the Constitution empowers the states to "appoint [electors], in such Manner as the Legislature thereof may direct.... " This grant of authority provides the constitutional basis claimed for the National Popular Vote initiative. In practice, all states currently provide for popular election of their electoral college delegations.[11] Candidates for the office of elector are nominated by political parties and other groups on the presidential ballot in each state. In most cases, the candidates for the office of elector are nominated by the state party committee or the party's statewide convention.[12] The winning presidential nominees must gain a national majority of 270 or more electoral votes, out of the 538 total, in order to be elected. If no ticket of candidates attains a majority, then the House of Representatives elects the President, and the Senate the Vice President, in a procedure known as contingent election.[13]

Candidates for the office of elector are selected by their respective political parties. They are expected to vote for the presidential and vice presidential candidates to whom they are pledged.[14] Some states seek to require them to so vote by law or other means, but most constitutional scholars hold that the electors remain free agents under the Constitution, and that they may vote for any person they choose.[15] On rare occasions, an elector will vote for a different candidate, or abstain from casting a vote for any candidate; he or she is known as a "faithless elector."[16]

The goal of presidential campaigns under the existing system is to win by carrying states that collectively cast a majority of electoral votes. Political parties and presidential campaigns tend to focus on states that are closely contested (widely referred to as "battleground" states), or that have large delegations of electoral votes, or both. Winning a majority of the more populous and/or battleground states is considered crucial to obtaining the necessary electoral vote majority.

In 48 states and the District of Columbia, the presidential/vice presidential ticket winning the most popular votes (a plurality or more) in that state is awarded all its electoral votes. That is to say, the winning party's entire ticket of electors is elected. This is referred to as the "winner-takeall" or "general ticket" system.[17]

Presidential Election Day is set by law for Tuesday after the first Monday in November every fourth year succeeding the election of President and Vice President.[18] On Presidential Election Day, voters cast *one* vote for the candidates they support. They are, however, actually voting for the state political party "ticket" of electors supporting those presidential and vice presidential candidates.[19] Presidential electors assemble on the first Monday after the second Wednesday in December following the general election.[20] They meet in their respective states, not collectively, and cast separate votes by ballot for the President and Vice President.[21] After the electors vote, the results are sent by the states to Congress and various other federal authorities. On January 6 of the year following a presidential election, Congress meets in a joint session to count the electoral votes and make a formal declaration of which candidates have been elected President and Vice President.[22]

THE NATIONAL POPULAR VOTE INITIATIVE: BACKGROUND[23]

A range of factors contributed to the emergence of the National Popular Vote initiative in the first decade of the 21st century. A major source was frustration by reform advocates after three decades of failed attempts to secure congressional approval for a direct popular election amendment. Perhaps a more immediate spur was the contentious and disputed presidential election of 2000, which is regarded as having been a major factor contributing to the development of the NPV proposal.

Electoral College Reform, 1948-1979: Three Decades of Unsuccessful Efforts to Propose a Constitutional Amendment

One of the factors cited for the emergence of the National Popular Vote initiative has been the exacting requirements set by the Constitution for amendments, in this case, a direct popular election constitutional amendment. As noted previously, approval by two-thirds of Members present and voting is required in both houses when Congress proposes an amendment, followed by ratification by three-fourths of the states, 38 at present, usually within a seven-year period specified by Congress. Between 1948 and 1979, Congress debated electoral college reform at length; throughout this time, hundreds of reform proposals were introduced in both chambers. They generally centered on one of two courses: "end it" by eliminating the entire electoral college system and establishing direct popular election, or "mend it" by reforming its more controversial provisions.[24] Between 1948 and 1979, proposed amendments were the subject of hearings in the Senate and House Judiciary Committees on 17 different occasions, while electoral college reform was debated in the Senate on five occasions and twice in the House during this period. Proposals were approved by the necessary two-thirds majority twice in the Senate and once in the House, but never in the same Congress.[25]

Following the 1979 defeat of a direct popular election amendment on the Senate floor, and the retirement or defeat of prominent congressional advocates, the question of electoral college reform largely disappeared from public attention and Congress's legislative agenda. Although Senators and Representatives continued to introduce reform proposals, few received action beyond routine committee referral, and in time, the number of measures introduced dropped to zero. Even after the presidential election of 2000, in which the winner of the electoral vote won fewer popular votes than his opponent (a so-called "misfire"), there was little evidence that Congress was prepared to consider an electoral college reform amendment.

Proposals to replace the electoral college system with direct popular election continued to be introduced, but in dwindling numbers as the years passed. In the 112th Congress, Representative Jesse L. Jackson Jr. introduced H.J.Res. 36, a direct popular election amendment, but at the time of this writing, no electoral college reform proposal has been introduced in the 113th Congress. By comparison, 41 direct popular election or electoral college reform amendments were proposed in the 95th Congress (1977-1978).

Survey Research: Public Support for Direct Popular Election

For the record, survey research findings have consistently identified broad support for direct popular election of the President and Vice President. In its most recent question on the issue, asked in 2013, the Gallup Poll reported that 63% of respondents favored an amendment providing for direct popular election, while 29% favored retention of the electoral college. This finding corresponds with similar levels of public approval recorded by Gallup since at least 1967.[26] Further, National Popular Vote, Inc., reports that statewide surveys in 38 states found similar support levels for direct popular election among respondents in 238 state polls taken between 2007 and 2011.[27]

It should be noted, however, that while these findings show support for direct popular election, they do not measure public commitment to the National Popular Vote initiative per se. At the time of this writing, it appears that no major survey research organization has sampled public opinion on the NPV plan, as opposed to general support for direct election.

The Election of 2000 and Electoral College Reform

The disputed presidential election of 2000 was arguably a catalyst for new thinking on electoral college reform. Following a closely contested campaign, Republican candidates George W. Bush and Richard Cheney were elected over Democratic nominees Al Gore Jr. and Joseph Lieberman following a bitter dispute over election results in Florida that was ultimately decided by the Supreme Court.[28] The High Court's decision left Bush and Cheney with a narrow plurality in Florida of 537 popular votes[29] and a similarly narrow electoral college majority of 30 states with 271 electoral votes, while their Democratic opponents took 20 states and the District of Columbia with 266 electoral votes (one District of Columbia elector cast a blank ballot in protest against the outcome). It was, moreover, the first election since 1888 in which the candidates elected uncontestably[30] won fewer popular votes than their principal opponents: the Gore/Lieberman Democratic ticket gained 50,992,335 popular votes to 50,455,156 for Bush/Cheney.[31]

These election results generated considerable discontent with the system. Some critics argued for a constitutional amendment, but the 107th Congress faced a heavy legislative burden throughout this period, which initially included enactment of President George W. Bush's legislative program and was later expanded to urgent responses to the terrorist attacks of September 11, 2001. Rather than focus on the lengthy process associated with consideration of a constitutional amendment, Congress focused on legislative remedies. The Help America Vote Act of 2002, passed in response to the numerous irregularities in voting systems and procedures revealed by the 2000 election, mandated election administration reforms and voting system technology enhancements (funded in part by federal grants to the states) intended to ensure accurate and timely voting and vote tabulation in future elections.[32]

Bypassing Constitutional Amendment Procedures to Attain Direct Popular Election: Emergence of the National Popular Vote Concept

While the 2000 election's "misfire" did not result in consideration of a constitutional amendment, it did prompt considerable study and investigation into new approaches to electoral reform among scholars and political activists of the presidential election process. Law professors Robert W. Bennett of Northwestern University, Vikram Amar of the University of California-Davis, and Akhil Amar of Yale University School of Law, are generally credited as the intellectual godparents of the concept that ultimately evolved into the National Popular Vote Interstate Compact,[33] which relies on the Constitution's broad grant of power to each state to "appoint, *in such Manner as the Legislature thereof may direct* [emphasis added], a Number of Electors, equal to the whole Number of Senators and Representatives to which the State may be entitled in the Congress."[34]

Project FairVote, an issue advocacy group self-described as a nonprofit, nonpartisan "501(c)(4)" organization, appears to have been an incubator of the National Popular Vote concept.[35] FairVote has supported NPV for "over a decade,"[36] and was an early supporter of National Popular Vote, Inc., the plan's official advocacy group;[37] moreover, longtime FairVote board members Robert Richie and former Representative John B. Anderson were early supporters of the National Popular Vote initiative and contributors to its manifesto, *Every Vote Equal.*[38]

THE NATIONAL POPULAR VOTE INITIATIVE (NPV)[39]

As noted previously, the National Popular Vote initiative (NPV) was the ultimate result of the various studies and proposals offered following the presidential election of 2000.

How the NPV Would Work

The National Popular Vote (NPV) initiative seeks to establish direct popular election of the President and Vice President through an interstate compact, rather than by constitutional amendment. Ideally, under the compact's provisions, legislatures of the 50 states and the District of Columbia would pass legislation binding the signatories to appoint presidential electors committed to the presidential/vice presidential ticket *that gained the most votes nationwide*. If all 50 states and the District of Columbia were compact members, this would deliver a unanimous electoral college decision for the candidates winning a plurality of the popular vote.

Specifically, the plan calls for an agreement among the states, an interstate compact effected through state legislation, in which the legislature in each of the participating states agrees to appoint electors pledged to the candidates who won the *nationwide popular vote*. State election authorities would count and certify the popular vote in each state, which would be aggregated and certified as the "nationwide popular vote." The participating state legislatures would then choose the slate of electors pledged to the "nationwide popular vote winner," *notwithstanding the results within their particular states.*[40] In order to insure success, the initiative would come into effect only if states whose total electoral votes equals or exceeds the constitutional majority of 270 were to approve the plan.

If the nationwide popular vote were effectively tied, the states would be released from their commitment under the compact, and could choose electors who represented the presidential ticket that gained the most votes in each particular state.

One novel NPV provision would enable the presidential candidate who won the national popular vote to fill any vacancies in the electoral college with electors of his or her own choice.

States would retain the right to withdraw from the compact, but if a state chose to withdraw within six months of the end of a presidential term, the withdrawal would not be effective until after the succeeding President and Vice President had been elected.

Managing the NPV Campaign: National Popular Vote, Inc.

The NPV advocacy effort is managed by National Popular Vote, Inc., a "501(c)(4)"[41] nonprofit corporation, established in California in 2006 by Barry Fadem, an attorney specializing in initiative and referendum law, and John R. Koza, Ph.D., an automated systems scientist and entrepreneur.[42] As a 501(c)(4) entity, it is permitted to engage in political activity in furtherance of its goal, without forfeiting its tax-exempt status, so long as this is not its primary activity. NPV states on its website that its "specific purpose is to study, analyze and educate the public regarding its proposal to implement a nationwide popular election of the President of the United States."[43] Dr. Koza serves as Chairman of NPV, Inc., and Mr. Fadem serves as President. In addition, Tom Golisano, an entrepreneur, philanthropist, and three-time candidate for governor of New York, is prominently featured on NPV's masthead.[44] In 2011, Mr. Golisano joined NPV, Inc., as a spokesman and major financial contributor. According to contemporary press accounts, Golisano was expected to be a spokesman for the National Popular Vote campaign who would "bankroll" NPV efforts.[45] NPV's advisory board includes former Senators and Representatives of both major political parties.[46]

In 2006, National Popular Vote, Inc., published a detailed handbook, *Every Vote Equal: A State-Based Plan for Electing the President by National Popular Vote*. This publication, in its fourth edition at the time of this writing, provides a detailed account of various issues related to the NPV initiative, including the electoral college, earlier reform efforts, interstate compacts, the text of the proposed compact, a strategy for advancing the initiative, and a 340-page section addressing "myths about the National Popular Vote Compact.[47]

National Popular Vote, Inc. maintains offices in Mountain View, CA, and Lady Lake, Fl.

Supporters in various state legislatures began to introduce measures to adopt the interstate compact shortly after NPV's inaugural press conference on February 23, 2006. The NPV Compact has been introduced in the legislatures of all 50 states and the Council of the District of Columbia, and has received active consideration in 26 states and the D.C. Council.

Among other activities, NPV maintains a regular communications program of e-mail newsletters announcing activities and soliciting readers to petition governors and state legislators to support the compact.[48] As of June 3, 2014, NPV claimed the support of 2,110 state legislators on its website, over one-sixth of the total of 7,382 legislators, and endorsements by the *New York Times*, *Los Angeles Times*, *Chicago Sun-Times*, *Minneapolis Star Tribune*, *Boston Globe*, *Miami Herald* and other newspapers.[49]

NPV also advocates use of the citizen initiative process where available to enact state adherence to the compact;[50] it asserts that when Article II, Section 1, clause 2 grants authority to the states to appoint "in such Manner as the Legislature thereof may direct," the authority extends to the states' entire law-making process, which in some states includes the proposal and passage of legislation and constitutional amendments through citizen initiative.[51] The citizen initiative approach to the interstate compact, however, has yet to be used at the time of this writing.[52]

States Adopting the National Popular Vote Interstate Compact, 2008-2014

As noted earlier, the National Popular Vote Interstate Compact has been introduced to date in the legislatures of all 50 states and in the Council of the District of Columbia.[53] As of the autumn of 2014, 10 states and the District of Columbia, possessing a total of 165 electoral votes, had adopted it. In chronological order with year of adoption, they are as follows:

- **Hawaii** (4 electoral votes), 2008;
- **Illinois** (20 electoral votes), 2008;
- **Maryland** (10 electoral votes), 2008;
- **New Jersey** (14 electoral votes), 2008;
- **Washington** (12 electoral votes), 2009;
- **Massachusetts** (11 electoral votes), 2010;
- **District of Columbia** (3 electoral votes), 2010;
- **Vermont** (3 electoral votes), 2011;

- **California** (55 electoral votes), 2011;
- **Rhode Island** (4 electoral votes), 2013; and
- **New York** (29 electoral votes), 2014.

After an initial momentum in 2008, when four states joined the compact in one year, NPV has made modest progress toward its goal of approval by states accounting for 270 electoral votes. Obvious highlights were California's approval in 2011, which added 55 electoral votes to the tally, and most recently, New York's accession to the compact, finalized by Governor Andrew Cuomo on April 15, 2014. This action added the Empire State's 29 electoral votes to the total and brought the NPV to 61% of its 270-vote operational threshold.[54]

At the time of this writing, the NPV compact had been actively considered in 2014 by six state legislatures: Arizona,[55] Connecticut,[56] Minnesota,[57] Oklahoma, where it was approved in the state Senate,[58] Michigan,[59] and Pennsylvania.[60] It remains to be seen whether New York's action will provide the impetus for further accessions in the near future, however, because the first four legislatures have adjourned for the year without taking action, leaving only Michigan and Pennsylvania in session through the balance of 2014. If the compact were approved by either of these states, which control 16 and 20 electoral votes respectively, NPV could arguably claim a "momentum" in its favor for the first time since 2008.

Conversely, proposals to rescind approval of the NPV Interstate Compact have been introduced in the legislatures of Hawaii, Maryland, Massachusetts, New Jersey, and Washington, to date, but none has been approved.[61]

Some observers note that, despite NPV's assertion of bipartisan support, all the jurisdictions that have joined the compact to date could be identified as "leaning" Democratic or "solid" Democratic in their support of the Democratic Party, as classified by a recent Gallup survey. For instance, nine of the 11, including California, the District of Columbia, Hawaii, Illinois, Maryland, Massachusetts, New Jersey, Rhode Island, and Vermont were found by Gallup to be among the "most solidly Democratic states in 2013." [62] Alluding to this fact, one commentator observed that

> All the states to have joined so far are very blue. Until some purple states and red states sign on, the compact has little in the way of territory to conquer.... The seven states where President Obama won [in 2012] by the widest margins, along with D.C., have joined. So have three others—New Jersey, Illinois and Washington—where

> Obama won by at least 15 percentage points. But none below that threshold have done so.[63]

Perhaps in response to perceived NPV momentum, defenders of the existing arrangements and the electoral college announced measures to promote retention of the electoral college system. December 7, 2011, of that year, the Heritage Foundation, a conservative public policy institute, hosted a forum at which guest speakers, including five state secretaries of state, expressed their concern over the National Popular Vote campaign.[64] That same month, *Roll Call* reported that the State Government Leadership Foundation, a project of the Republican State Leadership Committee, would begin a campaign to defend the electoral college and counter recent NPV gains.[65] Further activity, however, does not appear to have been undertaken by these groups at the time of this writing.

THE NATIONAL POPULAR VOTE INITIATIVE: PRO AND CON[66]

Arguments in support of and opposed to the National Popular Vote proposal resemble those advanced in favor of and against direct popular election of the President. The central issue turns on the question of the asserted simplicity and democratic attractiveness of the direct election idea as compared to a more complex array of factors cited by supporters of the electoral college system.

Arguments Favoring the NPV Compact

Proponents of the National Popular Vote initiative arguably share the philosophical criticism voiced by proponents of direct popular election, who maintain that the electoral college system is intrinsically undemocratic—it provides for "indirect" election of the President and Vice President. This, they assert, is an 18th century anachronism, dating from a time when communications were poor, the literacy rate was much lower, and the nation had yet to develop the durable, sophisticated, and inclusive democratic political system it now enjoys. They maintain that only direct popular election of the President and Vice President is consistent with modern democratic values and practice.

Beyond this fundamental challenge, critics cite what they identify as a wide range of technical failings of the electoral college arrangement. Perhaps the most prominent of these is that the electoral college system can result in the election of a President and Vice President who have won the electoral vote, but gained fewer popular votes than their major opponent. This condition results at least in part from to the nearly universal reliance on the "winner-take-all" or general ticket system of awarding electoral votes in the states, which is also criticized by NPV advocates. Under the general ticket system, the candidates winning the most popular votes in a state (a plurality is sufficient) are awarded *all* that state's electors and electoral votes; under these circumstances, a presidential ticket can gain all a state's electoral votes on even a slim margin of popular votes.[67] Presidents were elected in 1876, 1888, and 2000 who received fewer popular votes than their major party opponents, while the runner-up in both popular and electoral votes was elected by the House of Representatives when four candidates split the vote in the presidential election of 1824.[68]

NPV supporters advocate the compact on the grounds of fairness and respect for the voters' choice. At the core of their arguments, they assert that the process would be simple, national, and democratic; the NPV interstate compact would provide *de facto* for a single, democratic choice, allowing all the nation's voters to choose the President and Vice President directly, with no intermediaries. The "people's choice," they assert, would win in every election, and every vote would carry the same weight in the election, no matter where in the nation it was cast. No state would be advantaged, nor would any be disadvantaged. According to NPV, the central argument in favor is that the compact "would guarantee the Presidency to the candidate who receives the most popular votes [or at least a plurality] in all 50 states (and the District of Columbia)."[69] According to NPV, there would never again be a presidential election "misfire" or another "wrong winner."

Other elements of the electoral college system criticized by NPV advocates (and other electoral college reformers) would arguably disappear or be rendered irrelevant. These include the faithless elector phenomenon, the general ticket system's asserted "disfranchisement" of voters who backed the losing candidates, and various asserted "voting power" advantages attributed to large (populous) states, small states, states with large populations of noncitizens, states with low rates of voter participation, and populous states with concentrations of minority-group voters. In addition, the NPV compact would almost certainly eliminate the need for contingent election of the President and Vice President under the Twelfth Amendment.[70]

NPV advocates also assert the compact would provide a practical benefit to non-battleground "flyover" states. With "every vote equal," NPV maintains that presidential and vice presidential nominees and their organizations would need to spread their presence and resources more evenly as they campaigned for every vote nationwide, rather than concentrate on winning key "battleground" states. They assert that, under the present system,

> ... candidates have no reason to poll, visit, organize, campaign, or worry about the concerns of voters of states that they cannot possibly win or lose. This means that voters in two thirds of the states are effectively disenfranchised in presidential elections because candidates concentrate their attention on a small handful of "battleground" states. In 2004, candidates concentrated over two-thirds of their money and campaign visits in just five states; over 80% in nine states, and over 99% of their money in just 16 states.[71]

For instance, they note that California voters seldom see the presidential or vice presidential nominees or benefit from campaign spending because the Golden State, having voted Democratic since 1988, is considered to be reliably "blue," and Democratic Party candidates are said to take its 55 electoral votes for granted. They also note that Republican candidates make few California appearances, but for the opposite reason: why spend time and resources in support of an apparently hopeless cause. Similar arguments on the Republican side apply to Texas, a state that has voted for Republican presidential nominees since 1980. In 2012, for instance, neither presidential candidate, nor his vice presidential running mate, appeared in California or Texas during the general election campaign. By comparison, Ohio and Florida, closely contested battleground states, received, respectively, 73 and 40 candidate appearances.[72] According to *Every Vote Equal's* analysis of campaign appearances, the 2012 major party candidates for President and Vice President appeared at a total of 253 campaign events during the general election campaign, but they only visited 12 states; 38 states and the District of Columbia were bypassed during the campaign.[73]

NPV advocates also maintain that the concentration of campaign resources, advertising, and candidate appearances in battleground states depresses turnout in "flyover" states. *Every Vote Equal* notes that in 2012, voter participation in battleground states, as identified by political commentator Charles Cook, averaged 67%, while nationwide turnout averaged 59.4% in the nation as a whole.[74] The NPV manifesto further cites a Brookings Institution study of the 2004 presidential election in support of its argument,

"Because the electoral college has effectively narrowed elections like the last one to a quadrennial contest for the votes of a relatively small number of states, people elsewhere are likely to feel that their votes don't matter."[75] It should be noted, however, that a range of other political, social, cultural, and economic factors may also contribute to the disparity in turnout between battleground and non-battleground states.

NPV further suggests that the disparity in participation may ultimately damage the ability to govern on the state and local levels and could have a negative impact on the legitimacy of public institutions:

> Diminished voter turnout in presidential races in non-battleground states weakens down-ballot candidates, thereby making the state even less competitive in the future. Governance— not just electioneering—is affected by the winner-take-all rule.[76]

Arguments Opposing the NPV Compact

National Popular Vote opponents oppose the compact on various grounds. Some argue that it is unconstitutional or "anti-constitutional," i.e., contrary to the Founders' intentions and the spirit of the nation's fundamental charter. It is also asserted that NPV would solve few of the electoral college system's alleged problem issues and would create some of its own. Finally, some observers note that the NPV compact is an interstate compact as defined in Article I, Section 10, clause 3 of the Constitution, and as such would be subject to congressional approval. This issue is examined in greater detail in a separate section of this report.

On the most fundamental philosophical basis, opponents might argue that the National Popular Vote compact violates one of the basic principles of majoritarian democracy: it does not require that candidates win a *majority* of the popular vote in order to gain the presidency. Rather, it would anoint as winner the ticket that gains *more* popular votes than any other. A majoritarian democracy, it may be argued, should require a majority in order to elect; it may be further noted that the existing system, by comparison, requires a majority in the electoral college. As one commentary noted,

> ... only the strictest of majoritarians desire a purely majoritarian presidential election system, and those individuals should be deeply troubled by the prospect of plurality presidencies, which the NPVC [sic]expressly countenances. Indeed, the NPVC promises to create

> more difficulties and "misfires" in its own way than the Electoral College system its proponents so earnestly seek to replace.[77]

Further, opponents might ask how the National Popular Vote compact might function in the event of a multi-candidate election, a phenomenon that recurs from time to time in U.S. Presidential elections. One commentator posited a problematic scenario under such circumstances:

> Under the compact, one can easily imagine a multi-candidate race in which a candidate would win, say, a thirty-four percent plurality of the popular vote nationwide while losing in every state and D.C. If all of the states and D.C. were signatories to the compact, all the electoral votes in such a hypothetical race would be awarded contrary to the will of voters choosing electors (still not voting directly for President under this plan). Would the United States accept a President who wasn't the choice of sixty-six percent of those voting, nor even the choice of a single state?[78]

The existing electoral college system, NPV skeptics might also assert, is a fundamental element in the federal constitutional arrangements established by the Constitution. Fearing "the tyranny of the majority,"[79] the Founders established a system of government that provides checks and balances designed to restrain the majority and secure minority rights. These principles are also embedded in the structure of federal elections: the Senate, the House of Representatives and the presidency were given deliberately provided with different terms of office and different electorates and the states were given an important role in the federal election process. In particular, through the electoral college the United States elects its *national* Presidents and Vice Presidents in a state-based *federal* election. Successful nominees are compelled under this system to present a broad political vision that commands nation-spanning "concurrent majorities" and appeals to the great variety of Americans.[80] As in the case of the Senate, less populous states are assigned a small numerical advantage by assignment of two so-called senatorial electors to each state regardless of its population. The National Popular Vote initiative, they could claim, would discard the Founders' intentions in favor what they consider to be a flawed "majoritarian" presidency that would ill-serve a continent-spanning and profoundly diverse republic.

Another criticism centers on the use of the NPV compact to effect a fundamental change in the presidential election process and a *de facto* amendment to the Constitution, but without following the procedures set out in

Article V. Critics may note the NPV is described by its founders, as an admitted "end run" around the Constitution.[81] Proponents may argue that Article V presents too high a hurdle for what they consider a necessary reform of the system, but opponents would likely assert that the Founders intended the various super-majority requirements in Congress and the states to ensure that successful constitutional amendments enjoy broad national support. The bare majority of electoral votes required to implement NPV, they might note, meets none of these supermajority requirements. As one study critical of the NPV initiative concluded, the use of an interstate compact "does not conform to the constitutional means of changing the original decisions of the Framers, NPV could not [therefore] be a legitimate innovation."[82] A final argument on this line might be that one "end run" around the amendment process might lead to others, setting a dangerous precedent for similar efforts in the future.

Opponents might note that the NPV would eliminate the electoral college system's multiplier effect, which tends to magnify the winning ticket's margin of victory, and is said to confer greater legitimacy to the victors. For instance, in 2012, President Barack Obama won 50.16% of the popular vote, while his principal opponent, Mitt Romney, won 47.20%, a victory margin of 2.96%. Under the general ticket system, however, the President gained 332 electoral votes (67.71%) to Governor Romney's to 206 (38.29%). The multiplier effect increased the President's margin of victory in the electoral college by almost 800%, to an arguably decisive 23%.[83]

From a practical standpoint, NPV opponents might argue that the NPV would actually lead to an increase in contested election results and legal challenges in the states, as the political parties maneuver to claim every possible vote. They assert that the existing tabulation of popular votes within each state reduces contested results and recounts. Under NPV, the incentive to gain every vote would arguably lead to far broader disputes and widespread recounts at every level of election administration. As a Heritage Foundation study concluded,

> Under the NPV, however, any suspicions necessitating a recount in even a single district would be an incentive for a national recount.... The prospect of a candidate challenging 'every precinct, in every county, in every state of the Union' should be abhorrent to anyone who witnessed the drama, cost, delay, and undue litigation sparked by the Florida recount of 2000.[84]

The increased incidence of recounts would arguably be further complicated by wide-ranging disparities in state procedures, leading, potentially, to prolonged periods of uncertainty following close presidential elections.[85]

Critics may also note that the National Popular Vote plan contains no “statute of limitations,” unlike proposed constitutional amendments, for which Congress typically sets a seven-year ratification period.[86] Where, critics may ask, is a similar time limit that would “sunset” the National Popular Vote compact, after which it would expire or return to “square one?” According to its website, NPV was launched on February 23, 2006;[87] if it were a constitutional amendment, it would have expired on February 23, 2013, since by the end of the customary seven-year deadline it was “ratified” by only eight states and the District of Columbia. By what reasoning, they might argue, should the NPV be exempt from the standards of timeliness and contemporaneity Congress customarily sets for constitutional amendments?

Opponents might finally argue that NPV’s assertion that the compact would have the effect of spreading campaign spending resources and candidate events in non-battleground states is a questionable argument to justify a fundamental change in the presidential election process. Campaign appearances and spending, they might assert, moreover, should not be considered to be a local economic stimulus package, nor are the amounts in question sufficient to make much of a difference in the economic condition of most states. As one critical analysis notes, “... the nation does not hold presidential elections to foster local economic development.”[88] Moreover, they might continue, it is equally dubious to assert that nominees will slight the concerns of citizens of the non-battleground states from which they draw their greatest support, or that concentrated campaigning in the battleground states somehow “disenfranchises” voters in others. In the modern era, only a tiny percentage of voters actually sees a presidential or vice presidential candidate from either party. Television, especially broadcast and cable TV news networks, social media, the Internet, and newspapers, not the traditional rallies, torchlight parades and handbills, dominate presidential election campaigns in the 21st century.[89]

NATIONAL POPULAR VOTE: CONSTITUTIONAL AND LEGAL[90] ISSUES

In addition to policy issues discussed previously, some observers have also raised questions related to the National Popular Vote initiative based on the fact that it is an interstate compact as defined in the Constitution. Others have questioned whether NPV might interfere with some provisions of the Voting Rights Act.

The NPV Initiative As an Interstate Compact

The NPV initiative has been described by its supporters variously as a bill,[91] a state-level statute,[92] and an interstate compact.[93] The latter reference necessitates an analysis of whether the initiative complies with the Compact Clause of the Constitution.

An interstate compact—under the broadest understanding—is a contract between two or more consenting states.[94] The Supreme Court has further suggested that an interstate compact often requires reciprocal commitments between the governments of two or more states, such that one state's commitment is conditioned on the action of another state and no state can unilaterally repeal its commitment.[95] The use of interstate compacts predates the Constitution, because the Articles of Confederation contained a similar Compact Clause that provided a qualified prohibition on states entering into any agreements between them without the consent of Congress.[96] The chaos resulting from the disunity created by the Articles of Confederation prompted the Framers of the Constitution generally to "impose more uniformity" among the states,[97] resulting in a Constitution that *wholly* prohibits states from entering into any treaties, alliances, and federations.[98] Nonetheless, the Constitution maintained the Articles of Confederation's *qualified* prohibition on interstate compacts and agreements, allowing states to enter into an interstate compact so long as the participating states seek the consent of Congress.[99] Specifically, the Compacts Clause provides that "No State shall, without the Consent of Congress ... enter into any Agreement or Compact with another State...."[100] While the historical rationale for Article I's *qualified* prohibition on interstate compacts is unclear,[101] the Compact Clause generally reflects the view of the Framers that states should be able to work cooperatively together, as well as the concern that unchecked interstate alliances might threaten the harmony of the Union or the authority vested by the Constitution in the federal government.[102] As the Supreme Court noted, in *Cuyler v. Adams*, "(b)y vesting in Congress the power to grant or withhold consent, or to condition consent on the states' compliance with specified conditions, the Framers sought to ensure that Congress would maintain ultimate supervisory power over cooperative state action that might otherwise interfere with the full and free exercise of federal authority."[103]

Of note, the Compact Clause places no limits on what might be done through an interstate compact other than the requirement of congressional consent. In the early years of government under the Constitution, compacts were used almost exclusively to settle boundary disputes. Beginning with the establishment of the Port of New York Authority[104] in 1921, however, compacts began to be used to address more complex, regional issues requiring intergovernmental cooperation. Some compacts are merely advisory in form, but others may be regulatory, with significant powers granted to multi-state commissions.[105] More recently, compacts have addressed such wide-ranging concerns as mental health treatment, law enforcement and crime control, education, driver licensing and enforcement, environmental conservation, energy, nuclear waste control, facilities operations, transportation, economic development, insurance regulation, placement of children and juveniles, disaster assistance, and pollution control. Approximately 200 interstate compacts are in effect today.[106]

Accordingly, the central legal issue with respect to the Compact Clause is whether a given interstate compact requires the consent of Congress. While a "literal" reading of the Compact Clause "would require the States to obtain congressional approval before entering into *any* agreement among themselves, irrespective of form, subject, duration, or interest to the United States [emphasis added],"[107] the Supreme Court has repeatedly rejected such a reading. In 1893, in *Virginia v. Tennessee*,[108] Justice Stephen Field, writing for the Court, contended that a broad reading of the Compact Clause would "embrace all forms of stipulation, written or verbal, and relating to all kinds of subjects[,]"[109] requiring congressional consent to agreements "which the United States can have no possible objection or have any interest in interfering with," as well as those that "may tend to increase ... the political influence of the contracting states, so as to encroach upon or impair the supremacy of the United States.... "[110] Surmising that the Compact Clause could not have been intended to have such a broad reach,[111] Justice Field concluded that the Clause only prohibits states from entering into compacts without congressional consent when the underlying compact is "directed to the formation of any combination tending to the increase of political power in the States, which may encroach upon or interfere with the just supremacy of the United States."[112] The Supreme Court has subsequently reaffirmed Justice Field's "functional view of the Compact Clause,"[113] and, accordingly, generally where an agreement does not fall within the scope of Compact Clause as envisioned by the Court in *Virginia v. Tennessee,* the agreement "will not be invalidated for lack of congressional consent."[114]

Whether the NPV initiative requires congressional consent under the Compact Clause first requires a determination as to whether NPV even constitutes an interstate compact. At times, its supporters have resisted framing the initiative as an interstate compact, arguably out of concern for running afoul of the Compact Clause's provisions.[115] For example, Professor Akhil Amar has argued that because the initiative does not create a "new interstate governmental apparatus," the NPV should not be considered an interstate compact, as NPV compact signatory states are merely exercising power collectively that each state could exercise on its own.[116] It is unclear, however, whether the creation of a new interstate governmental entity formed out of an agreement between two or more states is necessary, as opposed to sufficient, in order to deem an agreement as being an interstate compact subject to the Compact Clause. While the Supreme Court, in *Northeast Bancorp*, suggested that a "joint organization or body" formed out of an interstate agreement is "classic indic[ium] of a compact,"[117] the Court has never adopted a definition of an interstate compact that solely rests on the existence of an interstate governmental body. Instead, the Court appears to have adopted a broader definition of what an interstate compact can entail. For example, in *Virginia v. Tennessee,* the Court noted that the words "compacts" and "agreements" are synonymous and "cover all stipulations affecting the conduct or claims of the parties."[118] In other words, when two or more states enter into a stipulated agreement whereby one state agrees to perform an act in consideration for a reciprocal act by the other state(s), that agreement can be considered an interstate compact.[119] This broad definition of a compact appears to encompass the NPV compact, as the initiative requires signatory states to agree mutually to appoint their electors to the winner of the national popular vote.[120] Moreover, NPV binds each assenting state, as no member state can withdraw from it within six months or less of the end of a President's term.[121] Because NPV prohibits states from freely "modify[ing] or repeal[ing] [the agreement] unilaterally" and requires "reciprocation" of mutual obligations,[122] it appears that the initiative can be described as an interstate compact.

Assuming the NPV initiative is an interstate compact, the question remains whether it is one that implicates the Compact Clause. The answer to that question primarily depends on whether NPV is "directed to the formation of any combination tending to the *increase* of political power in the States, which may *encroach upon or interfere* with the just *supremacy of the United States*."[123] In other words, the "test" for whether a particular interstate compact requires congressional consent is centrally concerned with *vertical* balances of power between the federal government and the states; namely "whether the Compact enhances state power *quoad* the National Government."[124] While the NPV arguably increases the political power of the states that have consented to it by ensuring that those states' desired outcome for the presidential election—the awarding of the majority of electoral votes to the presidential candidate supported by the majority of voting populace—it is unclear on how that increase in political power would be at the expense of the power of the federal government. After all, the Constitution provides the federal government with no role in determining the members of the electoral college.[125] One scholar has suggested that the NPV initiative would lead to a vertical alteration of power by eliminating the possibility that the House of Representatives would resolve a presidential election in the absence of an electoral majority for a single candidate because it is premised on a majority of electoral votes going to a single candidate.[126] The House of Representatives, however, has decided only two presidential elections in American history, and whether such an arguably hypothetical and *de miminis* diminishment of federal power through the NPV would be sufficient to require congressional consent under the Compact Clause is simply unresolved by the relevant case law.[127]

While the Supreme Court's case law interpreting the Compact Clause is centrally concerned with *vertical* federalism concerns (i.e., the balance of power between the state and federal governments),[128] the Court has not explicitly rejected a potential secondary rationale suggested for the Compact Clause: to preserve the *horizontal* balance of powers among the various states.[129] And horizontal federalism concerns could very well be implicated by the Compact Clause, as the provision appears to have been included in the Constitution out of concern both for the supremacy of the federal government *and* unity among the various states.[130] Whether the NPV compact threatens the powers of nonconsenting states has been the subject of much debate among academics. Those in support of the initiative have contended that the nonconsenting states do not lose any power as a result of the NPV.[131] According to this line of argumentation, even under the NPV, all states would retain their right to select the electors of their choosing, as nonmember state electors would still be counted in the electoral vote.[132] Others, however, have pointed to the underlying premise of the NPV—to enhance the political power of more populous states in presidential elections—as evidence that the initiative diminishes the power of nonconsenting states.[133] In other words, while non-compacting states would still retain the power to appoint electors, the influence that comes with that power would arguably be diminished because a state's role in the national election would be defined by its percentage of the popular vote and not by its percentage of electors, warranting congressional interest in approving a compact that effectuated such a change in national elections.[134] Ultimately, however, whether horizontal federalism concerns are truly implicated by the Compact Clause and whether the NPV actually threatens the power of nonconsenting states is a debate that remains active within academia but would likely be the source of considerable litigation if the initiative ever became effective.[135]

If congressional consent is needed for the NPV, that consent can take various forms. Usually congressional consent to an interstate compact takes the form of a joint resolution or act of Congress specifying its approval of the text of the compact and adding any conditions or provisions it deems necessary, often embodying the compact document. As with most congressional actions, consent to an interstate compact must occur with the approval of both houses and must be signed by the President before it becomes law.[136] Very rarely has the President vetoed or threatened to veto consent legislation by Congress.[137] While congressional consent to an interstate compact is most often explicit, consent by Congress may also be implied by subsequent acts of Congress as "[a]n inference clear and satisfactory that Congress ... intended to consent" to a compact may be sufficient.[138] Congress may also delegate its power to approve a compact to a federal official so long as an "intelligible principle" against which approval can be measured is apparent.[139] Ultimately, if congressional consent is truly needed for NPV to be effective, the initiative might have difficulty ever being enacted because the approval of both houses of Congress and the President would likely necessitate additional hurdles beyond the already challenging task of amassing support at the state level for the NPV.[140]

The NPV Initiative and Article II of the Constitution

Beyond the legal issues raised with respect to the Compact Clause, the NPV initiative also potentially raises other broader constitutional concerns, including whether the states can functionally obviate the role of the electoral college through the NPV. Article II of the Constitution establishes that the election of the President should occur *indirectly* through the election by the electoral college.[141] The choice of an *indirect* election for the President was a deliberate one by the Framers of the Constitution, because, while noting the importance that the "sense of the people" should influence the choice for

President,[142] they found it "equally desirable" for the "immediate election" of the President to be made by a body representative of distinct state interests and removed from the threat of unchecked majoritarianism.[143] The result was that the Constitution established a presidential election process that was "manifestly nonmajoritarian,"[144] with the electoral college, a body established to represent the distinct views of each state, as the centerpiece of the election process.[145] The central constitutional issue presented by the NPV, therefore, is whether the states, through an interstate compact, can functionally transform the presidential election system enshrined in the Constitution into a more majoritarian process.

Supporters of the NPV argue that the Constitution provides the legal means for states to transform the presidential election system into one where the President is elected based solely on the result of the national popular vote. Specifically, clause two of Article II, Section one of the Constitution provides the states with the power to "appoint, in such Manner as Legislature therefore may direct," the electors who represent the state in the electoral college.[146] Facially, the Constitution's primary limitation on the power of a state to select its electors is the final number of electors awarded to each state.[147] While perhaps an argument can be made that the structure, logic, and history of the Constitution place limits on the manner or method in which a state chooses its electors, the text of the Constitution simply does not impose any such limits.

Supreme Court case law also supports reading Article II of the Constitution to *broadly* provide states with wide discretion as to the manner in which its electors are selected. Specifically, in 1892 in *McPherson v. Blacker,* a unanimous Supreme Court upheld a Michigan law providing for the election *by individual congressional district* of presidential electors against a challenge that the law violated Article II of the Constitution.[148] In so holding, the Court placed great emphasis on a number of state laws that existed shortly after the ratification that provided a variety of "modes of choosing the electors," including selection by the legislature itself, by a "vote of the people for a general ticket," "by vote of the people in districts," or by some permutation of those methods.[149] Viewing this evidence together with the text of Article II[150] and the historical evidence from the Constitutional Convention[151] led the Court to broadly conclude state legislatures have "conceded plenary power ... in the matter of the appointment of electors,"[152] allowing the Michigan law to stand. Applying *McPherson* to the case of the NPV, the argument can and has been made that if the states have plenary power with respect to the manner of how electors are appointed, the power necessarily allows states to select electors in line with the results of the national popular vote.[153]

Others have argued that the structure of the Constitution and historical evidence suggests that the states do not have such vast discretion in appointing electors as to functionally transform the election for President into a national popular referendum.[154] As noted elsewhere in this report, the electoral college was created by the Framers to ensure that states with the least population retained power in the selection of the President, providing a check against domination by the most populous states.[155] The electoral college, being a product of the choices of individual state legislatures, was envisioned by the Framers as a body that would represent the specific interests of a given state, as opposed to the undifferentiated nation at large.[156] Accordingly, it may be argued that allowing the most populous states to collude to ensure that the national popular vote, as opposed to the wishes of an individual state, dictate the results of a state's slate of electors, could arguably be irreconcilable with the Framers' intentions with respect to the electoral college.[157]

As such, for those who find the NPV compact constitutionally suspect under Article II, *McPherson*'s broad pronouncements about the nature of a state's power to appoint electors should be viewed in the context of that particular case, where the State of Michigan was attempting to appoint its electors based on the votes of an individual district in the state, as opposed to the state as a whole. In contrast to the law at issue in *McPherson*, with NPV, there appears to be no evidence contemporaneous with the ratification of the Constitution of a state selecting its electors in accordance with the results of the *national* popular vote. Unlike the State of Michigan in *McPherson,* an NPV state's electors might not be a product of the views of the state at the time of the election, but instead would reflect national popular sentiment about who should be the President. Moreover, the Supreme Court, in interpreting arguably analogous language from Article I of the Constitution allowing states to regulate the manner of the selection of the members of the House of Representatives and Senate,[158] concluded that the states cannot exercise their delegated authority in a way that would "effect a fundamental change in the constitutional structure."[159] The question that remains is whether the Court in a future case challenging the NPV compact would interpret the states' authority under Article II to appoint electors to be broad enough to allow the President to be selected as a result of the national popular vote, a question that, given the lack of any precise precedent respecting the constitutionality of the NPV compact under Article II, will likely remain unresolved until such time.[160]

The NPV Compact and the Voting Rights Act[161]

Other critics claim the National Popular Vote compact might violate Sections 2 and 5 of the Voting Rights Act (VRA). Writing in *Columbia Law Review*, David Gringer invokes the voting power theory.[162] He argues that the plan conflicts with Section 2 of VRA because moving from "a state-based [vote] to a national popular vote dilutes the voting strength of a given state's minority population by reducing its ability [voting power] to influence the outcome of presidential elections."[163]

Gringer also asserts that the NPV compact may violate Section 5 of the act.[164] In 2013, however, the U.S. Supreme Court invalidated Section 4(b) of the VRA,[165] which contained a formula prescribing which states and jurisdictions with a history of discrimination were required to obtain prior approval or "preclearance" under Section 5 before changing any voting standard, practice, or procedure.[166] Although the Court invalidated only the coverage formula in Section 4, by extension, Section 5, has been rendered currently inoperable. Prior to the Supreme Court ruling, Gringer argued that the NPV compact would qualify as a covered practice under Section 5, and that the legislatures of all the "covered" states would have been required to obtain preclearance before implementing the compact.[167]

Responding to this point, National Popular Vote, Inc., noted that

> The National Popular Vote bill manifestly would make every person's vote for President equal throughout the United States in an election to fill a single office (the Presidency). It is entirely consistent with the goal of the Voting Rights Act. There have been court cases under the Voting Rights Act concerning contemplated changes in voting methods for various representative legislative bodies.... However, these cases do not bear on elections to fill a single office (i.e., the Presidency).[168]

It should, however, be noted that in 2012, the Justice Department's Civil Rights Division specifically declined to challenge California's accession to the NPV compact on Voting Rights Act grounds.[169]

Finally, it may be noted that the states' authority to appoint electors by any method their legislatures choose is not absolute. Federal court decisions have struck down state laws concerning appointment of electors that were found to be in violation of the Fourteenth Amendment's guarantee of equal protection:

> Although Clause 2 (of Article II, Section 1 of the Constitution) seemingly vests complete discretion in the states, certain older cases had recognized a federal interest in protecting the integrity of the process. Thus, the Court upheld the power of Congress to protect the right of all citizens who are entitled to vote to lend aid and support in any legal manner to the election of any legally qualified person as a presidential elector.... [I]n *Oregon v. Mitchell* (42 U.S. 112 (1970)), the Court upheld the power of Congress to reduce the voting age in presidential elections and to set a thirty-day durational residency period as a qualification for voting in presidential elections. Although the Justices were divided on the reasons, the rationale emerging from this case, considered with *Williams v. Rhodes*, (393 U.S. 20 1968)) is that the Fourteenth Amendment limits state discretion in prescribing the manner of selecting electors and that Congress in enforcing the Fourteenth Amendment may override state practices that violate that Amendment and may substitute standards of its own.[170]

CONCLUSION

Critics of the electoral college system have sought direct election of the President and Vice President without success for close to two centuries. The National Popular Vote initiative represents a novel effort to achieve this goal by use of an interstate compact which would circumvent the stringent requirements necessary for the proposal and ratification of constitutional amendments.

Since its inception in 2006, NPV has achieved a degree of success: 10 states and the District of Columbia, controlling a total of 165 electoral votes, have joined the compact since 2008. Progress has arguably been sporadic, however, notwithstanding active campaigning by National Popular Vote, Inc. When populous states like California and New York have joined the compact, the results have been widely publicized: additional state approvals are predicted, and opponents sound the alarm; but NPV has yet to develop a sustained momentum toward its stated goal of states controlling 270 electoral votes. To date, only Democratic-leaning states[171] have joined the compact. This evident lack of support in Republican-controlled state legislatures arguably raises questions about further accessions to the compact in the immediate future, particularly given the fact that the GOP will control both legislative chambers in 29 states in 2015.[172]

To date, while the National Popular Vote initiative has generated interest among supporters of direct popular election of the President, it does not appear to have gained widespread awareness or support in the public at large. This could change, however, if NPV were to develop sustained momentum, and if more states were to join the compact, particularly populous ones like Pennsylvania (20 electoral votes) and Michigan (16 electoral votes), where the NPV compact was received legislative consideration in 2014.[173] Under these circumstances, proponents might be energized and encouraged by the sense of progress, while at the same time, opponents could be expected to coalesce around the issues identified earlier in this report, and the activities of both might bring the National Popular Vote initiative to the more immediate attention of Congress.

End Notes

[1] Thomas H. Neale is the author of this section.

[2] In "presidential" republics, the President customarily serves as chief executive, exercises considerable authority, and is generally elected by popular vote. Mexico, Brazil, and France are examples of presidential republics, although France also provides for a prime minister who is responsible to the legislature. In "parliamentary" republics, the President customarily serves as ceremonial head of state and is generally elected by indirect vote. Executive authority is usually vested in the office of the head of government, known variously as prime minister, premier, or chancellor. Germany, India, and Israel are examples of parliamentary republics.

[3] Alexander Hamilton, "The Method of Electing the President," in *The Federalist*, Number 68 (Cambridge, MA: The Belknap Press of the Harvard University Press, 1961), p. 440.

[4] "U.S. Electoral College, Frequently Asked Questions," National Archives website, at http://www.archives.gov/ federal-register/electoral-college/faq.html#changes.

[5] Article V provides two avenues for amendment of the Constitution, proposal by Congress, as noted above, and proposal by a convention summoned by the applications of two-thirds of the states. For additional information on the Article V Convention alternative, please consult, CRS Report R42589, *The Article V Convention to Propose Constitutional Amendments: Contemporary Issues for Congress*, by Thomas H. Neale, and CRS Report R42592, *The Article V Convention for Proposing Constitutional Amendments: Historical Perspectives for Congress* , by Thomas H. Neale.

[6] Thomas H. Neale is the author of this section.

[7] 3 U.S.C. §4.

[8] U.S. Constitution, Article II, Section 1.

[9] Ibid., 23rd Amendment.

[10] Ibid., Article II, Section 1.

[11] Neal Peirce and Lawrence Longley, *The People's President, The Electoral College in American History and the Direct Vote Alternative*, rev. ed. (New Haven: Yale University Press, 1981), pp. 44-47.

[12] See U.S. Congress, Senate, *Nomination and Election of the President and Vice President of the United States, 2008*, "Part IV. State Laws Relating to the Nomination and Election of Presidential Electors." S. Doc. 111-15 (Washington: GPO, 2010), pp. 346-444.

[13] For more detailed information on the contingent election process, please consult CRS Report R40504, *Contingent Election of the President and Vice President by Congress: Perspectives and Contemporary Analysis*, by Thomas H. Neale.

[14] Ibid.

[15] See *U.S. Constitution, Analysis and Interpretation, "The Constitution Annotated,"* Article II Analysis, Article II, Section 1, clauses 2-4, "Election: Electors as Free Agents," available online to Members of Congress and staff at http://crs.gov/conan/default.aspx?mode=topic&doc=Article02.xml&t=1|4&s=1&c=2.

[16] For further information, see Peirce and Longley, *The People's President*, pp. 99-102.

[17] Maine and Nebraska use a different method of allocating electoral votes, the "district" system, under which votes are counted twice: on a statewide basis, and on a congressional district basis. The ticket receiving the most votes statewide receives two electoral votes for this total. The ticket winning the most votes in each congressional district receives a single electoral vote for each district it wins. In this way, a state's electoral vote may be divided to reflect geographical differences in support within the state for different candidates.

[18] 3 U.S.C. §1.

[19] For individual state provisions, see *Nomination and Election of the President and Vice President*, pp. 310-345.

[20] 3 U.S.C. § 7.

[21] U.S. Constitution, Article II, Section 1; 12th Amendment. The words "by ballot" are interpreted to mean by paper ballot. With respect to the location of meetings of the electors, the Founders reasoned that if they met in their respective states, there would be less opportunity for political intrigue and chicanery than if they assembled in a single location. The difficulties inherent in long-distance travel at the time may also have influenced the Constitutional Convention's decision.

[22] 3 U.S.C. §15-18. The same sections of the *U.S. Code* provide for challenges to electoral votes, as occurred in 2001 and 2005.

[23] Thomas H. Neale is the author of this section.

[24] The three principal reform proposals would all eliminate the office of elector, and distribute electoral votes on the basis of different criteria. They were, and remain: (1) the automatic system, which would award electoral votes "automatically" in each state on a winner-take-all basis; (2) the district system, which would incorporate the system currently in place in Maine and Nebraska; and (3) the proportional system, which would award votes in each state in direct proportion to the percentage of popular votes won by competing tickets in that state.

[25] For a detailed examination and analysis of these efforts, see Peirce and Longley, *The People's President*, pp. 131- 206.

[26] Lydia Saad, "Americans Call for Term Limits, End to Electoral College, Would Swap Electoral College for Popular Vote," *The Gallup Poll*, January 18, 2013, at http://www.gallup.com/poll/159881/americans-call-term-limits-endelectoral-college.aspx.

[27] "Polls Show More Than 70% Support for a Nationwide Vote for President," National Popular Vote website, at http://nationalpopularvote.com/pages/polls.php.

[28] *Bush v. Gore*, 531 U.S. 98 (2000).

[29] Richard M. Scammon, Alice V. McGillivray, and Rhodes Cook, *America Votes 24, A Handbook of Contemporary American Politics* (Washington: CQ Press, 2001), p. 120.

[30] In 1960, a controversy arose over counting of votes for Democratic Party electors in Alabama. Some analysts maintained that vote totals for nominee John F. Kennedy were overstated, and that a more accurate accounting would have reduced his total in the state, giving Republican nominee Richard M. Nixon a slim nationwide popular vote plurality of 58,181 votes. See Peirce and Longley, *The People's President*, pp. 63-73.

[31] Scammon, McGillivray, and Cook, *America Votes 24*, p. 9.

[32] The Help America Vote Act, 116 Stat. 1666. For additional information, please consult CRS Report RS20898, *The Help America Vote Act and Election Administration: Overview and Issues*, by Kevin J. Coleman and Eric A. Fischer.

[33] Robert W. Bennett, "Popular Election of the President Without a Constitutional Amendment," in *The Green Bag, An Entertaining Journal of Law*, 4 Green Bag 2d 241, available from the Social Science Research network by subscription, see http://papers.ssrn.com/sol3 /papers.cfm?abstract_id=261057; Akhil Reed Amar and Vikram David Amar, "How to Achieve Direct National Election of the President without Amending the Constitution," *Findlaw's Writ*, December 28, 2001, at http://writ.news.findlaw.com /amar/20011228.html.

[34] U.S. Constitution, Article II, Section 1, clause 2.

[35] FairVote, founded in 1982 as Citizens for Proportional Representation, which later became the Center for Voting and Democracy, seeks to educate and enliven "discourse on how best to remove the structural barriers to democracy." FairVote's portfolio also includes such initiatives as "voter preregistration for young people, universal voter registration, a constitutional right to vote, and fair representation voting forms of proportional registration." FairVote.org, "Who We Are," at http://www.fairvote.org/who-we-are/who-we-are-2/.

[36] FairVote, "Time for National Popular Vote, not Electoral College Rigging," at http://www.fairvote.org/news/timefor-national-popular-vote

[37] FairVote, "About FairVote–Center for Voting and Democracy," at http://archive.fairvote.org /about_us/.

[38] John R. Koza et al., *Every Vote Equal: A State-Based Plan for Electing the President by National Popular Vote*, 4th ed. (Los Altos, CA: National Popular Vote Press, 2014).

[39] Thomas H. Neale is the author of this section.

[40] Under NPV, assume that presidential ticket "A" won 55% of the popular vote in State "X," and ticket "B" won 45%. Under the current general ticket system, the state legislature would typically choose electors pledged to ticket A. Under NPV, assume the same in-state results, but assume that ticket "B" won the national popular vote. The state legislature, in compliance with the National Popular Vote compact, would vote to choose electors committed to ticket "B," because that ticket won the national popular vote, notwithstanding the in-state returns.

[41] 26 U.S.C. 501 (c)(4). Nonprofit tax-exempt organizations recognized by the Internal Revenue Service under this provision of the IRS Code often lobby for legislation and participate in political campaigns and elections.

[42] Rick Lyman, "Innovator Devises Way Around Electoral College," *New York Times*, September 22, 2006, at http://www.nytimes.com/2006/09/22/us/politics

[43] National Popular Vote, Inc., website, "About," at http://www.nationalpopularvote.com /pages/about.php.

[44] Ibid.

[45] Joseph Spector, "Tom Golisano to Lead National Popular Vote Effort," *WGRZ.com* (Buffalo, New York), February 23, 2011, at http://www.wgrz.com/news/article/110466/1/Tom-Golisano-to-Lead-National-Popular-Vote-Effort. Hendrik Hertzberg, "N.P.V. Gets a

Boost," *The New Yorker* (Blogs), March 14, 2011, at http://www.newyorker.com/online/blogs/hendrikhertzberg/2011/03/npv-gets-a-boost.html .

46 Advisory Board members listed on the NPV, Inc., website include former Representatives John Anderson, John Buchanan, Tom Campbell, and Tom Downey and former Senators Birch Bayh, David Durenberger, and Jake Garn, and a separate category of "champions" that includes former Senators Fred Thompson and Chet Culver, and former Representative Jim Edgar. See NPV, Inc., website at http://www.nationalpopularvote.com/pages/about.php.

47 Koza et al., *Every Vote Equal: A State-Based Plan for Electing the President by National Popular Vote*, 4th ed..

48 National Popular Vote, Inc., website, "Newsletters," at http://www.nationalpopularvote.com /pages/newsletters.php.

49 National Popular Vote, Inc., website, "Home," at http://www.nationalpopularvote.com /index.php.

50 Koza et al., *Every Vote Equal*, pp. 293-294. There is no evidence at the time of this writing that the initiative process has been successfully invoked to place National Popular Vote proposals on state ballots.

51 Ibid., see Chapter 8, pp. 297-341.

52 Initiative and Referendum Institute, "Ballotwatch," at http://www.iandrinstitute.org /ballotwatch.htm.

53 National Conference of State Legislatures website, at http://www.ncsl.org/research/elections-and-campaigns national-popular-vote.aspx.

54 Ibid., "Home," at "https://www.governor

55 Arizona: in committee when the special legislative session adjourned May 29, 2014. National Conference of State Legislatures website, "2014 Legislative Session Calendar," at http://www.ncsl.org/research/about-state session-calendar-2014.aspx.

56 Connecticut: passed in committee and pending when the legislative session adjourned May 9, 2014. Connecticut General Assembly website, at http://www.cga.ct.gov/asp/cgabillstatus /cgabillstatus.asp?selBillType=Bill&bill_num= HB05126&which_year=2014.

57 Minnesota: tabled in the House, Minnesota State Legislature website, at https://www.revisor.mn.gov/bills/bill.php? b=House&f=HF0799&ssn=0&y=2013&ls=88; in committee in the Senate; legislature adjourned May 16, 2014 at https://www.revisor.mn.gov/bills/bill.php?f=SF585&y=2013&ssn=0&b=senate.

58 Oklahoma: passed Senate, referred to House committee. Legislature adjourned May 30, 2014. Oklahoma State Legislature website, at http://www.oklegislature.gov/BillInfo.aspx?Bill=SB906&Session=1400.

59 Michigan: Active, in Senate committee; legislature normally remains in session through the end of the year. Michigan Legislature website, at http://www.legislature.mi.gov/(S(kyesuf45i1k13rvtjsr1iuyb))/mileg.aspx?page=getObject&objectName=2013-SB-0291.

60 Pennsylvania: referred to committee in House; legislature normally remains in session through the end of the year. Pennsylvania General Assembly website, at http://www.legis.state

61 National Conference of State Legislatures website, at http://www.ncsl.org/research/elections-and-campaigns national-popular-vote.aspx.

62 Lydia Saad, "Not As Many U.S. States Lean Democratic in 2013," Gallup Politics, January 29, 2014, at http://www.gallup.com/poll/167030/not-states

63 Nate Silver, "Why a Plan to Circumvent the Electoral College is Probably Doomed," *Five Thirty Eight*, April 17, 2014, at http://fivethirtyeight.com/datalab/why-a-plan-to-circumvent-the-electoral-college-is-probably-doomed/.

[64] Heritage Foundation, "The Electoral College and the National Popular Vote Plan," at http://www.heritage.org/events/ 2011/12/electoral-college.

[65] Eliza Newlin Carney, "GOP Nonprofit Backs Electoral College," *Roll Call.com*, December 8, 2011, at http://www.rollcall.com/issues. For further information on the State Government Leadership Foundation and its election law-related activities, see the foundation's website at, http://www.sglf.org /election-law.

[66] Thomas H. Neale is the author of this section.

[67] For instance, President Barack Obama won Florida in 2012 with 50.01% of the popular vote to Governor Mitt Romney's 49.13%. Under the winner-take-all system, the President won all 29 of Florida's electoral votes, notwithstanding the closeness of the popular vote contest. Conversely, Governor Romney won 50.39% of North Carolina's popular vote to the President's 48.35%, but won all 15 of North Carolina's electoral votes. Source: Federal Election Commission, *Official 2112 General Presidential Election Results*, January 17, 2013, at http://www.fec.gov/ pubrec/fe2012/2012presgeresults.pdf.

[68] This was a contingent election, since no candidate won a majority of electoral votes. For more information, see above.

[69] National Popular Vote website, at http://www.nationalpopularvote.com/pages/explanation.php.

[70] For further information, see above at footnote 10.

[71] National Popular Vote website, at http://www.nationalpopularvote/com/pages/explanation.php.

[72] Koza, et al., *Every Vote Equal*, p. 34.

[73] Ibid.

[74] Ibid., p. 37.

[75] Pietro S. Nivola, "Thinking About Political Polarization," The Brookings Institution, Policy Brief #139, January 2005, at http://www.brookings.edu/research/papers/2005/01/01politics-nivola.

[76] Koza, et al., *Every Vote Equal*, p. 38.

[77] Norman R. Williams, "Reforming the Electoral College: Federalism, Majoritarianism, and the Perils of Subconstitutional Change," *Georgetown Law Review*, vol.100, issue 1, 2011, p. 173.

[78] Alexander S. Belenky, "The Good, the Bad, and the Ugly, Three Proposals to Introduce the Nationwide Popular Vote in U.S. Presidential Elections," *Michigan Law Review*, June 2014, vol. 112, at http://www.michiganlawreview.org/ articles/the-good-the-bad-and-the-ugly-three-proposals-to-introduce-the-nationwide-popular-vote-in-u-s-presidentialelections.

[79] See especially James Madison, "The Size and Variety of the Union as a Check on Faction," Federalist 10, in *The Federalist* (Cambridge, MA: the Belknap Press of Harvard University Press, 1967), pp. 129-136.

[80] Daniel P. Moynihan, "The Electoral College and the Uniqueness of America," in *Securing Democracy, Why We Have an Electoral College*, ed., Gary L. Gregg, II (Wilmington, DE: ISI Books, 2001), pp. 91-93.

[81] This is the term applied by NPV founder, John Koza, in a 2006 interview: "When people complain that it's an end run," Dr. Koza said, "I just tell them, 'Hey, an end run is a legal play in football.'" Rick Lyman, "Innovator Devises Way Around Electoral College," *New York Times*, September 22, 2006, at http://www.nytimes.com/2006/09/22/us/ politics/22electoral.html.

[82] John Samples, *A Critique of the National Popular Vote Plan for Electing the President*, Cato Institute, Policy Analysis No. 622, October 13, 2008, p. 9.

[83] U.S. Federal Election Commission, *Federal Elections 2012*, pp. 5-6, at http://www.fec.gov/pubrec/fe2012/ federalelections2012.pdf.

[84] Hans von Spakovsky, *Destroying the Electoral College: The Anti-Federalist National Popular Vote Scheme*, Heritage Foundation Legal Memorandum No. 73, October 26, 2011, p.8.

[85] Samples, *A Critique of the National Popular Vote Plan for Electing the President*, p. 11.

[86] Congress has set the seven-year period as a reasonable time limit for the ratification process for the 18th and 20th through 26th Amendments.

[87] See National Popular Vote website, at http://www.nationalpopularvote.com /pages/summary.php.

[88] Samples, *A Critique of the National Popular Vote Plan for Electing the President*, p. 11.

[89] For instance, see Jeff Zeleny, "The Up-Close-and-Personal Candidate? A Thing of the Past," *New York Times*, November 30, 2011, at http://www.nytimes.com/2011/12/01/us /politics/presidential-candidates-make-fewer-in-personappearances.html?_r=0.

[90] Andrew L. Nolan is the author of this section.

[91] "Explanation of the National Popular Vote Bill," National Popular Vote website, at http://www.nationalpopularvote.com/pages/explanation.php#exp_1page.

[92] "What Is the National Popular Vote Plan?: Facts and FAQs," FairVote.org website, at http://www.fairvote.org/ reforms/national-popular-vote/what-is-the-national-popular-vote-plan/.

[93] "Explanation of the National Popular Vote Bill," National Popular Vote website, at http://www.nationalpopularvote.com/pages/explanation.php#exp_1page.

[94] See *Texas v. New Mexico*, 482 U.S. 124, 128 (1989) (noting that a "Compact is, after all, a contract.") (quoting Petty v. *Tennessee-Missouri Bridge Comm'n*, 359 U.S. 275, 285 (1959) (Frankfurter, J., dissenting)).

[95] See *Northeast Bancorp v. Bd. of Governors of Fed. Reserve Sys.*, 472 U.S. 159, 175 (1985) (*dicta*). The *Northeast Bancorp* Court further noted that an interstate compact often entails the existence of a "joint organization or body" overseeing the agreement. *Id.*

[96] Articles of Confederation, Article VI ("No two or more States shall enter into any treaty, confederation or alliance whatever between them, without the consent of the United States in Congress assembled, specifying accurately the purposes for which the same is to be entered into, and how long it shall continue.").

[97] Adam Schleifer, "Interstate Agreement for Electoral Reform," *Akron Law Review*, vol. 40, issue 1, 2007, pp. 717,728-729.

[98] U.S Constitution, Article I, Section 10, clause 1.

[99] Ibid., Article I, Section 10, clause 3.

[100] Ibid.

[101] See *United States Steel Corp v. Multistate Tax Commission*, 434 U.S. 452, 463 (1978) ("Whatever distinct meanings the Framers attributed to the terms in Art. I, § 10, those meanings were soon lost.").

[102] Michael L. Buenger and Richard L. Masters, "The Interstate Compact on Adult Offender Supervision: Using Old Tools to Solve New Problems," *Roger Williams Law Review*, vol. 9, issue 1, fall 2003, pp.71, 85.

[103] 449 U.S. 433, 439-440 (1981).

[104] 1921 N.Y. Laws Ch. 154; N.J. Laws Ch. 151; 42 Stat 174 (1921).

[105] Administrators under compacts with congressional compacts with congressional consent may have the power to promulgate rules and regulations and may also review federal agency action under certain circumstances. See *Seattle Master Builders Assn. v. Pacific Northwest Elec. Power*, 786 F.2d 1359, 1362 (9th Cir. 1986).

[106] Council of State Governments, National Center for Interstate Compacts (NCIC), at http://www.csg.org/programs/ ncic/default.aspx. The NCIC website includes a database of current interstate compacts searchable by state, name of compact, and subject.

[107] See *United States Steel Corp.*, 434 U.S. at 459.

[108] 148 U.S. 503 (1893).

[109] Ibid. at 517-518.

[110] Ibid. at 518.

[111] Ibid. Justice Field listed four examples of interstate agreements that could in "no respect concern the United States:" (1) an agreement by one state to purchase land within its borders owned by another state; (2) an agreement by one state to ship merchandise over a canal owned by another; (3) an agreement to drain a malarial district on the border of two states; and (4) an agreement to combat an immediate threat, such as invasion or an epidemic.

[112] Ibid. at 519.

[113] *United States Steel Corp.*, 434 U.S. at 468; see also *New Hampshire v. Maine*, 426 U.S. 363, 369 (1976) ("The application of the Compact Clause is limited to agreements that are 'directed to the formation of any combination tending to the increase of political power in the States, which may encroach upon or interfere with the just supremacy of the United States.'"); *Northeast Bancorp*, 472 U.S. at 175-76 (same).

[114] See *Cuyler v. Adams*, 449 U.S. 433, 440 (1981). It should be noted, however, that the consent power of Congress is absolute. Congress can require consent to any interstate compact and can deny consent to any interstate compact if it so chooses. This may be true even where affirmative consent is not necessary. *St. Louis & San Francisco Ry. Co. v. James*, 161 U.S. 545 (1896); *Petty v. Tennessee-Missouri Bridge Commission*, 359 U.S. 275 (1959). See also *Cuyler v. Adams*, 449 U.S. 433 (1981), where the Court deferred to Congress's political judgment that the Interstate Agreement on Detainers was to be treated as a compact pursuant to the Compact Clause even if the Constitution did not require such treatment. Justice White noted that the "requirement that Congress approve a compact is to obtain its political judgment." *Cuyler*, 449 U.S. at 441, n. 8 (White, J., dissenting).

[115] See, e.g., Robert Bennett, "California Bill Could Spur Changes in How We Elect President: A New Movement Is Afoot to Institute a National Popular Vote," *Chicago Sun Times*, September 30, 2006, p. 14. ("First, calling the measure an interstate compact is neither necessary nor wise. The constitution says that congressional approval is required for an 'agreement or compact' among states. Though this requirement might not be applicable to the present effort, the chance should not be taken.").

[116] See Akhil Reed Amar, "Some Thoughts on the Electoral College: Past, Present, and Future," *Ohio Northern University Law Review*, vol. 33, no. 2, 2007, pp. 467, 478.

[117] 472 U.S. at 175.

[118] 148 U.S. at 520.

[119] Ibid. ("The legislative declaration will take the form of an agreement or compact when it recites some consideration for it from the other party affected by it, for example, as made upon a similar declaration of the border or contracting State. The mutual declarations may then be reasonably treated as made upon mutual considerations. The compact or agreement will then be within the prohibition of the Constitution.... ")

[120] See *"Agreement Among the States to Elect the President by National Popular Vote,"* Article. III, at http://www.nationalpopularvote.com/pages/misc/888wordcompact.php ("The chief election official of each member state shall designate the presidential slate with the largest national popular vote total as the 'national popular vote winner.'").

[121] Ibid. Article IV ("Any member state may withdraw from this agreement, except that a withdrawal occurring six months or less before the end of a President's term shall not become effective until a President or Vice President shall have been qualified to serve the next term.").

[122] *Northeast Bancorp,* 472 U.S. at 175.

[123] *Virginia,* 148 U.S. at 519 (emphasis added).

[124] *Multi-State Tax Comm'n,* 434 U.S. at 473.

[125] U.S. Constitution, Article II, Section 1.

[126] Schleifer, "Interstate Agreement for Electoral Reform," pp. 739-740. Another commentator has argued that the "NPV is clearly a threat to federal supremacy since it would replace a federal institution established by the Constitution with a popular vote system." Ian J. Drake, "Federal Roadblocks: The Constitution and the National Popular Vote Interstate Compact," Publius, The Journal of Federalism, 10.1093/publius/pjt037 PUBLIUS: THE J. OF FEDERALISM 9 (2013)

[127] It should be noted, however, that the Supreme Court in *Multi-State Tax Commission* did agree that the "pertinent inquiry [with respect to the Compact Clause] is one of potential, rather than actual, impact on federal supremacy." *Multi-State Tax Comm'n,* 434 U.S. at 472. Arguably, the potential for an erosion of the House of Representative's authority necessitates congressional consent.

[128] Ibid., at 473 ("But the test is whether the Compact enhances state power *quoad* the National Government."); see also *New Hampshire v. Maine*, 426 U.S. 363, 369 (1976) (quoting *Virginia* v. *Tennessee,* 148 U.S. at 519) ("The application of the Compact Clause is *limited* to agreements that are 'directed to the formation of any combination tending to the increase of political power in the States, which may encroach upon or interfere with the just supremacy of the United States.'") (emphasis added).

[129] Jennifer S. Hendricks, "Popular Election of the President: Using or Abusing the Electoral College?" *Election Law Journal*, vol. 7, issue 3, 2008, pp. 218-225. ("[T]he Court's focus on federal concerns is a happenstance of the cases and arguments that have come before it. The Court has never *rejected* state interests as a factor in deciding whether to require congressional consent to a compact."). The Court has, at times, assumed the premise that the Compact Clause is concerned with preserving the rights of States that are not members to a particular compact. *Multi-State Tax Comm'n,* 434 U.S. at 477 ("Appellants' final Compact Clause argument charges that the Compact impairs the sovereign rights of nonmember States ... We find no support for this conclusion."); see also *Northeast Bancorp,* 472 U.S. at 176 ("Petitioners also assert that the alleged regional compact impermissibly offends the sovereignty of sister States outside of New England. We do not see how the statutes in question either enhance the *political* power of the New England States at the expense of other States or have an 'impact on our federal structure.'") (emphasis in original and internal citations omitted).

[130] See above, footnotes 90-95 and accompanying text.

[131] Hendricks, "Popular Election of the President: Using or Abusing the Electoral College?" p 226.

[132] Ibid., ("Complaining that some of those choices will not count because the NPV states would have enough votes to control the Electoral College is akin to current complaints that Democratic votes in Texas or Republican votes in California 'don't count.' Being in the minority does not mean that your vote is not counted; it just means that you lose."); see also Schleifer, "Interstate Agreement for Electoral Reform," pp.740-41 ("'any judgment of 'enhancement' [of member states' power] requires a baseline for comparison.' Setting this

baseline at today's distribution of electoral clout seems legally arbitrary – today's distribution is not a matter of legal right or inherent constitutional architecture, but is instead an accident of demographics.") (internal citations omitted).

[133] *See* Derek T. Muller, "The Compact Clause and the National Popular Vote Interstate Compact," *Election Law Journal*, vol.6, no. 4, 2007, pp. 372, 392; see also Drake, "Federal Roadblocks: The Constitution and the National Popular Vote Interstate Compact," p. 7. ("[The member states] will be the de facto group that actually elects the president.... Thus, the NPV compact 'tend[s] to increase and build up the political influence of the contracting states' in relation to the non-contracting states."). Adam Schleifer raises an additional argument that *member* states' power would be diminished under the NPV, as "[s]tates as political units are no longer making electoral decisions on their own, but are instead linking those decisions to the undivided citizenry." See Schleifer, "Interstate Agreement for Electoral Reform," p. 740.

[134] Derek T. Muller, "More Thoughts on the Compact Clause and the National Popular Vote: A Response to Professor Hendricks," *Election Law Journal*, vol. 7, no. 3, 2008, pp. 227,231. ("While the ultimate *outcome* of the election may not be pre-determined, the ability of states to *participate* in the political process with effective electoral votes and to wield political power *has* been pre-determined. Non-compacting states and their electors are left on the outside.") (emphasis in the original).

[135] Drake, "Federal Roadblocks: The Constitution and the National Popular Vote Interstate Compact," p. 17. ("It is likely that if and when the requisite number of states have enacted the NPV compact there will be multiple suits filed in state and federal courts seeking injunctions against states' implementation of the compact.").

[136] See *Metropolitan Wash. Airports Auth. v. Citizens for Abatement of Aircraft Noise*, 501 U.S. 252, 276 (1991) ("If the power is legislative, Congress must exercise it in conformity with the bicameralism and presentment requirements of Art. I, § 7."); see also ibid. at 276, footnote 21 (citing the limited provisions of the Constitution which permit Congress or a part of Congress to take some actions without complying with the bicameral and presentment requirements of Article I, Section 7 of the Constitution, without citing the Compact Clause).

[137] In 1942, President Franklin D. Roosevelt vetoed the Republican River Compact, stating that it "seeks to withdraw the jurisdiction of the United States over the waters of the Republican Basin for purposes of navigation." *Congressional Record*, vol. 87, pt. 3, April 2, 1941, pp. 3285-3286. He did, however, sign a later, modified version of the compact. See 57 Stat. 86, also, Joseph F. Zimmerman, *Interstate Cooperation: Compacts and Administrative Agreements*, 2nd ed. (Albany, NY: State University of New York Press, 2012), p. 56.

[138] *Virginia v. West Virginia*, 78 U.S. 39, 60 (1870). Congressional consent "is always to be implied when Congress adopts the particular act by sanctioning its objects and aiding in enforcing them.... " *Virginia,* 148 U.S. at 521.

[139] *Milk Indus. Found. v. Glickman*, 132 F.3d 1467, 1471 (D.C. Cir. 1998).

[140] Ian J. Drake, "Move to Diminish Electoral College Faces Constitutional Roadblocks," The Constitution Center, September 20, 2013, at http://blog.constitutioncenter.org/2013/09 /move-to-diminish-electoral-college-facesconstitutional-roadblocks/ ("Thus, the dilemma facing NPV proponents: the NPV compact must be submitted to Congress but cannot be approved by Congress.")

[141] U.S. Constitution, Article II, Section 1, clause 2.

[142] Hamilton, "The Method of Electing the President," in *The Federalist*, Number 68, p. 440.

[143] Ibid., p. 441. See also Norman Williams, "Why the National Popular Vote Compact is Unconstitutional," *Brigham Young University Law Review*, vol. 2012, issue 5, pp. 1523, 1549. Professor Williams of Willamette University provides an overview of the historical foundation for the electoral college in this article, noting that a proposal at the Constitutional Convention that the President be elected by "citizens of [the] U.S." drew "substantial opposition."

[144] Williams, "Why the National Popular Vote Compact is Unconstitutional," p. 1577.

[145] U.S. Constitution, Article II, Section 1, clause 2.

[146] Ibid.

[147] Ibid. As noted earlier in this report, the Constitution prohibits a Senator, Representative, or any "Person holding an Office of Trust or Profit under the United States" from serving as an elector.

[148] 146 U.S. 1, 23 (1892).

[149] Ibid., at 29-33 (surveying the laws of the various states from the nation's early history).

[150] Ibid., at 27 (noting the word "appoint" in Article II, Section 1, clause 2 was "manifestly used as conveying the broadest power of determination.").

[151] Ibid., at 28 (reading the Journal of the Convention to conclude that the Framers intended to "leav[e] it to the state legislatures to appoint directly by joint ballot or concurrent separate action, or through popular election by districts or by general ticket, or as otherwise might be directed.").

[152] Ibid., at 35 ("[T]he power and jurisdiction of the State is exclusive.... "); see also Ibid. at 27 ("[The Constitution] recognizes that the people act through their representatives in the legislature and leaves it to the legislature exclusively to define the method of effecting the object."); *Bush v. Gore*, 531 U.S. 98, 104 (2000) ("[A] State legislature's power to select the manner for appointing electors is plenary; it may, if it so chooses, select the electors itself.").

[153] See, e.g. Vikram David Amar, "Response: The Case for Reforming Presidential Elections by Subconstitutional Means: The Electoral College, the National Popular Vote Compact, and Congressional Power," *Georgetown Law Journal*, vol. 100, issue 1, 2011, pp. 237, 251, (rejecting that "no single state could ever take account of the vote tally in any other state as any kind of meaningful factor in the process for allocating its electors" because such an argument is inconsistent with the concept that states have plenary power "to determine the manner of selecting electors.").

[154] Williams, "Why the National Popular Vote Compact is Unconstitutional," p. 1577.

[155] Ibid., pp. 1577-1579.

[156] Hamilton, "The Method of Electing the President," in *The Federalist*, Number 68, p. 441. ("And as the electors, chosen in each State, are to assemble and vote in the State in which they are chosen, this detached and divided situation will expose them much less to heats and ferments, which might be communicated from them to the people, than if they were all to be convened at one time, in one place.").

[157] See Williams, "Why the National Popular Vote Compact is Unconstitutional," pp.1577-1578. This may be especially true given the historical evidence that the concept of a national popular vote was "overwhelmingly defeated" at the Constitutional Convention.

[158] U.S. Constitution, Article I, Section 3, clause 1, ("The Times, Places, and Manner of holding Elections for Senators and Representatives, shall be prescribed in each State by the Legislator thereof.... ").

[159] *United States Term Limits v. Thornton*, 514 U.S. 779, 837 (1995), (holding that "important changes in the electoral process" must occur "through the amendment procedures set forth in Article V.").

[160] In addition to constitutional questions respecting the Compact Clause and Article II, Section 1, clause 2, others have suggested that NPV would violate the Guarantee Clause of Article IV, see Kristin Feeley, "Comment: Guaranteeing a Federally Elected President," *Northwestern University Law Review*, vol. 109, no. 3, 2009, pp. 1427, 1459. ("NPV legislation violates the structural principle that no state should legislate for any other state. Placing no constitutional limit on state power over electors also creates the dangerous potential for eleven states to form a superstate and render the remaining thirty-nine states irrelevant in the election of the President. The limitations the Guarantee Clause provides against these results are desirable.") and the Fourteenth Amendment's Equal Protection Clause; see Williams, "Reforming the Electoral College: Federalism, Majoritarianism, and the Perils of Subconstitutional Change," p. 173. ("Simply aggregating votes from each of the fifty states and District of Columbia raises severe problems under the Equal Protection Clause of the Fourteenth Amendment."). Given the dearth of case law and scholarly debate on the Guarantee Clause and the Equal Protection Clause in even a related context to the NPVcompact, however, these topics are outside the scope of this report.

[161] L. Paige Whitaker, Legislative Attorney in the American Law Division of the Congressional Research, provided counsel and assistance in preparing this section.

[162] As noted earlier, the voting power theory holds that a state's influence depends on the size of its electoral college delegation, and its consequent ability to influence the outcome of an election. For a fuller explanation of voting power, see Lawrence D. Longley and Neal R. Peirce, *The Electoral College Primer 2000* (Yale University Press, New Haven: 1999), pp. 149-161.

[163] David Gringer, "Why the National Popular Vote Plan is the Wrong Way to Abolish the Electoral College, *Columbia Law Review*, vol. 108, 2008, p. 208.

[164] 42 U.S.C. §1973c.

[165] 42 U.S.C. §1973b.

[166] See *Shelby County v. Holder*, 133 S. Ct. 2112 (2013). For further discussion of the Supreme Court ruling, see CRS Report R42482, *Congressional Redistricting and the Voting Rights Act: A Legal Overview*, by L. Paige Whitaker.

[167] Gringer, "Why the National Popular Vote Plan is the Wrong Way to Abolish the Electoral College," p.188.

[168] National Popular Vote, *Myths About the National Popular Vote*, "20.1, 20.2 Myths About the Voting Rights Act," at http://www.nationalpopularvote.com/pages/answers /section. php?s=20.

[169] U.S. Department of Justice, Civil Rights Division, Letter of T. Christian Herren, Jr., Chief, Voting Rights Section, at, http://www.fairvote.org/assets

[170] *United States Constitution: Analysis and Interpretation (The Constitution Annotated)*, Article II, Section 1, Clauses 2-4, at http://www.crs.gov/conan/details.aspx?mode=topic&doc= Article02.xml&t=1|2&s=1&c=2.

[171] As defined in a recent Gallup Poll. See Lydia Saad, "Not as Many U.S. States Lean Democratic in 2013," *Gallup Politics*, January 29, 2014, at http://www.gallup.com/poll/167030/not-states

[172] John Blosser, "GOP Wins 'Historic Opportunity' to Move Agenda at State Level," Newsmax.com, November 6, 2014, at http://www.newsmax.com/Politics/Republicans-GOP-power-state

[173] 2014 Legislative Session Calendar, NCSL, National Conference of State Legislatures, at http://www.ncsl.org/ research/about-state-legislatures/session-calendar-2014.aspx.

In: Proposals for Presidential Election Reform ISBN: 978-1-63482-933-5
Editor: Maureen Stone

Chapter 2

ELECTORAL COLLEGE REFORM: CONTEMPORARY ISSUES FOR CONGRESS*

Thomas H. Neale

SUMMARY

The electoral college method of electing the President and Vice President was established in Article II, Section 1 of the Constitution, as revised by the Twelfth Amendment. It provides for election of the President and Vice President by electors who are themselves elected by the voters. A majority of 270 of 538 electoral votes is necessary to win.

The electoral college has been the subject of reform proposals since 1800. Constitutional and structural criticisms have centered on several of its features: it is not fully democratic, providing indirect election of the President; it can lead to the election of candidates who win the electoral college but fewer popular votes than their opponents or to contingent election in Congress if no candidate wins an electoral college majority; it results in electoral vote under- and overrepresentation between censuses; and that "faithless" electors can vote against the people's express choice. Legislative and political criticisms include the general ticket system, currently used in all states except Maine and Nebraska, which is said to disenfranchise voters who prefer the losing candidates in the states; various asserted "biases" that are alleged to favor different states and groups; and the electoral college "lock," which was once claimed to

* This is an edited, reformatted and augmented version of a Congressional Research Service publication, No. R43824, dated December 12, 2014.

provide an advantage to Republican candidates, but is now said to favor Democrats.

Electoral college reform options include the following: end it, mend it, or leave it alone. Proposals to end the electoral college almost always propose direct popular election, with the candidates winning the most popular votes nationwide elected. Almost all reform proposals would eliminate electors and award electoral votes directly by one of several methods: the general ticket system; the district system that awards electoral votes on a congressional-district and statewide-vote basis; and the proportional system that awards state electoral votes in proportion to the percentage of popular votes gained by each candidate. Despite more than 30 years of legislative activity from the 1940s through the late 1970s, proposed amendments never managed to win the constitutionally required two-thirds vote in both houses of Congress.

Since 2004, some of the reforms identified above have been attempted in the states. District plan initiatives have been offered in California, Pennsylvania, Michigan, Virginia, and Wisconsin. Proportional plans have been proposed in Colorado and Pennsylvania. Nebraska has considered returning to the general ticket system. None of these, however, has been enacted to date.

A nongovernmental organization is currently promoting the National Popular Vote (NPV) initiative, an interstate compact that would effectively achieve direct popular election of the President and Vice President without a constitutional amendment. It relies on the Constitution's grant of authority to the states in Article II, Section 1, to appoint presidential electors "in such Manner as the Legislature thereof may direct.... " States that join the compact pledge to award their electoral votes to the nationwide popular vote winners, regardless of who wins in their particular states. The compact would come into effect only after states controlling a majority of electoral votes (270 or more) were to join it. In April 2014, New York joined the compact, generating renewed interest in the NPV initiative. At the time of this writing, 10 states and the District of Columbia, which jointly control 165 electoral votes, have joined the NPV compact.

INTRODUCTION

The United States is unusual among contemporary presidential republics in that it provides for the indirect election of its President and Vice President.[1] Election of these two officers by a group of electors, known collectively as the electoral college, was established in Article II, Section 1 of the U.S. Constitution. The states were given blanket authority to appoint these electors "in such Manner as the Legislature[s] thereof" may direct. The original constitutional provisions, under which electors cast two votes for different candidates for President, but none for Vice President, proved unworkable[2] after only two contested elections,[3] leading to a constitutional crisis during the deadlocked election of 1800.[4] Following this event, Congress proposed the Twelfth Amendment, which provides for separate ballots for these two officials, and which was ratified by the states in time for the 1804 election. The presidential election provisions of Article II, Section 1 and the Twelfth Amendment have remained unchanged since that time.

As with other provisions of the Constitution, Article II, Section 1 and the Twelfth Amendment provided a basic framework for presidential elections, but left considerable leeway as to its implementation. In the years following ratification of the Twelfth Amendment, state laws and political party procedures added a range of now-familiar additional elements to the system. These include such practices as

- popular election of electors by the voters;
- joint tickets for presidential and vice presidential candidates—the voter casts a single ballot for both candidates;
- the predominance of the general ticket, or winner-take-all, method, which awards all of a state's electoral votes to the ticket that wins the most popular votes statewide;
- a broad range of nomination procedures for elector candidates; and,
- an enduring tradition that electors are expected, but not constitutionally required, to vote for the candidates to whom they are pledged.

The electoral college system has proved to be durable: 53 presidential elections have been held under this arrangement since the Twelfth Amendment was implemented in 1804. In 52 of these, it delivered a majority of electoral votes for President and Vice President, [5] and in 49 instances it delivered the presidency to "the people's choice," the candidates who won the most popular votes.[6] When measured by the first factor—delivery of a majority to one candidate or ticket—the electoral college has a success rate of 98.1%; when measured by whether it has delivered the presidency to "the people's choice," it enjoys a success rate of 92.4%. The electoral college has never been beyond criticism, however. Proposals to reform its alleged failings, or to replace it with something completely different, have been offered since the earliest days of the republic.

THE ELECTORAL COLLEGE IN BRIEF: A PRIMER

Origins of the Electoral College at the Constitutional Convention

Few questions so vexed the Constitutional Convention of 1787 as that of presidential election. During the convention, the delegates voted successively for election by Congress; direct popular election by the people; selection by the governors of the several states; election by electors chosen by the state legislatures; and even election by a group of Members of Congress chosen by lot.[7] At length, the matter was referred to a committee on "postponed matters," which reported a compromise plan near the close of the convention. The committee considered a range of generally agreed-upon principles for choice of the chief executive. Proceeding from the lengthy convention debate on choosing the chief executive, they contrived a mode of election designed to

- be free of undue influence by Congress, thus insuring greater independence in the executive and separation of powers;
- provide a fundamental role for the states by establishing the election as a federal, as well as a national, process;
- allocate electors by a formula that provided a certain degree of advantage to less populous states, to avoid complete domination of the election process by the more populous ones;
- give the state legislatures broad authority over the choice of electors: at the legislatures' discretion, electors could be picked by popular vote, by the legislature itself, or by another body altogether; and, ultimately
- temper popular enthusiasms and partisan and sectional attachments by giving the actual vote to the electors, who, it was hoped, would be prominent citizens of their states and communities, well-informed and educated persons who would make a balanced and measured selection.

Notwithstanding the Founders' intentions, from the very beginning, the electoral college began to change, evolving through constitutional amendment, state laws, and political party practices. The growth of political parties and the spread of voting rights and democratic principles overtook the Founders' vision that the President would be chosen by the nation's most distinguished citizens within two decades, as the electoral college evolved into the compound system that continues to govern U.S presidential elections two centuries later.

The Contemporary Electoral College System by the Numbers

As noted previously, the U.S. Constitution's minimal electoral college provisions have been complemented over the past two centuries by a range of federal and state laws, political party procedures, and enduring political traditions, leading to the system as it exists today. The salient features of the contemporary arrangement, a mixture of these elements, are detailed below.

- The electors are collectively known as the electoral college; although this phrase does not appear in the Constitution, it gained currency in the early days of the republic, and was recognized in federal law in 1845.[8]
- The electoral college has no continuing existence. Its sole purpose is to elect the President and Vice President; electors convene in the state capitals, vote, and adjourn.
- Each state is allocated a number of electors equal to the combined total of its U.S. Senate and House of Representatives delegations;[9] in addition, the District of Columbia is also allocated three electors.[10] At present, the total is 538, reflecting the combined membership of the Senate (100 Members), the House (435 Members), and the District of Columbia electors.
- Any person may serve as an elector, except Senators and Representatives, or any other person holding an office of "trust or profit" under the United States.[11]
- As noted previously, the state legislatures select the method by which electors are chosen.[12] In practice, all states currently provide for popular election of their electoral college delegations.[13] Candidates for the office of elector are nominated by political parties and other groups eligible to be on the ballot in each state. In most cases, the elector candidates are nominated by the state party committee or the party's state convention.[14]
- The winning presidential and vice presidential candidates must gain a majority of electoral votes (270 of 538) to be elected.

- If no ticket of candidates attains a majority, then the House of Representatives elects the President and the Senate elects the Vice President, in a procedure known as contingent election.[15]

How the Electoral College Functions in Contemporary Elections

- Presidential election day is set by federal law for Tuesday after the first Monday in November every fourth year succeeding the election of President and Vice President; one-third of U.S. Senators, all Members of the House of Representatives, and many state and local officials are also chosen on election day, which falls on November 8 in 2016.[16]
- On election day, voters across the country cast *one* vote for the team of presidential and vice presidential candidates they support. When they do so, they are actually voting for the political party "ticket" of candidates for the office of elector who support, and pledge to vote for, that party's presidential and vice presidential candidates.
- The popular vote is cast and certified, the electors are chosen, and they then vote in their respective states. While the nationwide popular vote count, the "horse race," is generally accorded widespread publicity during the campaign, ultimately it is the electoral vote tally in the states that decides the election.
- The goal of presidential campaigns is to win by carrying states that collectively cast a majority of electoral votes. In particular, political parties and presidential campaign organizations focus on states that are closely contested, that have large delegations of electoral votes, or both. Winning a majority of the more populous of these "battleground states"[17] is considered crucial to obtaining the necessary electoral vote majority.
- In 48 states and the District of Columbia, the ticket that wins the most popular votes, a plurality or more, is awarded all the state's electoral votes. That is, the winning party's entire slate or ticket of candidates for the office of elector is elected. This is referred to as the "general ticket" or "winner-take-all" system.
- Maine and Nebraska use a different method, the "district" system, under which popular votes are counted twice, first, on a statewide basis, and second, on a congressional district basis. The presidential/vice presidential ticket receiving the most votes *statewide*

receives two electors (or electoral votes) for this total. The ticket winning the most votes *in each congressional district* receives a single elector/electoral vote for that district. In this way, a state's electoral vote may be divided to reflect geographical differences in support within the state for different candidates.[18]

- Presidential electors assemble on the first Monday after the second Wednesday in December following the election.[19] In 2016, the electors are to assemble on December 19. They meet in their respective states and cast separate votes by secret paper ballot for the President and Vice President.[20]
- As noted earlier, candidates for the office of elector are selected by their respective political party. They are expected to vote for the candidates to whom they are pledged, but occasionally, a "faithless elector" will vote against instructions.[21]
- After the electoral college votes, the results are forwarded by state officials to Congress and various other federal authorities designated by law. On January 6 of the year following a presidential election, Congress meets in a joint session to count the electoral votes and make a formal declaration of which candidates have been elected President and Vice President.[22]

ELECTORAL COLLEGE ISSUES

As noted in the introduction to this report, the electoral college and the system built around it have delivered a President and Vice President in 52 of 53 elections since the Twelfth Amendment was ratified in 1804. It has elected the candidates who received the most popular votes in 49 of those elections. While the system's defenders point to this as a considerable achievement, the electoral college has been criticized for a wide range of alleged failings since the earliest days of the republic. These criticisms fall generally in one of two categories. The first is essentially *philosophical*, and centers on the fact that the existing system is indirect, and provides a lessthan-fully democratic indirect election of the President and Vice President. The second category addresses perceived constitutional, legislative, and political *structural* flaws in the system, focusing on its potential for various dubious procedures and outcomes, and the "biases" it is alleged to confer on certain groups and jurisdictions.

Philosophical Criticism: The Electoral College Provides Indirect Election of the President

Perhaps the fundamental contemporary criticism of the Founders' creation is philosophical. Proponents of change maintain that the electoral college system is intrinsically undemocratic—it provides for "indirect" election of the President and Vice President. They assert that this is an 18th century anachronism, dating from a time when communications were poor, the literacy rate was much lower, and the nation had yet to develop the durable, sophisticated, and inclusive democratic political system it now enjoys. They maintain that only direct popular election of the President and Vice President is consistent with modern democratic values and practice. Survey research consistently shows broad popular support for direct election.[23] In its most recent question on the issue, asked in January 2013, the Gallup Poll reported that 63% of respondents favored an amendment providing for direct popular election, while 29% favored retention of the electoral college. This finding mirrors those recorded by Gallup as early as 1967.[24]

Defenders of the electoral college system reject this suggestion; they maintain that while it may be indirect, it is not undemocratic—electors are chosen by the voters in free elections. They argue that the system prescribes a federal election of the President with votes tallied in each state, noting that the United States is a federal republic, not a plebiscitary democracy. The states, they assert, are long-established entities: distinct political, social, and economic communities that exercise substantial authority in many areas of governance, including presidential elections. The Founders, they note, intended that choosing the President would be an action Americans take both as citizens of the United States and as members of their state communities.[25]

Structural Criticisms of the Electoral College System

Beyond the fundamental claim that the electoral college is undemocratic, critics also cite what they identify as a wide range of structural flaws in the system; some of these are asserted to have origins in the constitutional provisions authorizing the electoral college system, while others are attributed variously to state legislation and political party practices.

Constitutional Issues

Some of the electoral college system's asserted failings are attributed by its critics to its structure and provisions as established in Article II, Section 1 of the Constitution and the Twelfth Amendment.

The Minority President: An Electoral College "Misfire"

Perhaps the most widely cited structural criticism of the electoral college system is that it can lead to the election of Presidents and Vice Presidents who carry enough states to win a majority of the electoral vote, but who have gained fewer popular votes nationwide than their major opponents. This result has been variously referred to as "wrong winner"[26] or an electoral college "misfire," and has occurred four times in the nation's history, in 1824, 1876, 1888, and most recently in 2000.[27] Proponents of direct election claim this potential violates a fundamental democratic principle that the candidate winning the most popular votes should be elected. Electoral college supporters defend the system on the grounds that it is a federal election rather than a national plebiscite, and further note the system has delivered "the people's choice" in 49 of 53 elections since ratification of the Twelfth Amendment, a success rate of 92.4%, as noted earlier in this report.

Failure to Gain an Electoral College Majority: Contingent Election

Contingent election, the electoral college "default" setting for cases in which no candidate receives the necessary majority of electoral votes, has also been cited as a structural failing of the system. If the presidential and/or vice presidential candidates fail to receive a simple majority of the electoral college votes, the Twelfth Amendment to the Constitution provides that the House of Representatives chooses the President and the Senate chooses the Vice President by contingent election.[28] In a contingent election, however, each state casts a single vote for President in the House, while each Senator casts a single vote for Vice President.[29]

Critics of the contingent election system generally argue that it further removes the choice of President and Vice President from the voters. That is, members of the House and Senate are free to exercise their choice without regard to the winners of the popular vote in their districts, states, or in the nation at large. Moreover, by effectively granting each state an equal vote, they claim that contingent election fails to account for great differences in population—and the number of votes cast—in the various states. Finally, it may be noted that the Twelfth Amendment does not provide for District of Columbia participation in a contingent election in the House and Senate.

While the ratification of the Twenty-third Amendment in 1961 granted the District of Columbia three votes in the electoral college, the nation's capital would be effectively disenfranchised in a contingent election, as it is not a state and sends neither Senators nor Representatives to Congress.

Defenders might counter by noting that contingent election is a "break glass only in case of an emergency" procedure, and has been required only once, under arguably unique circumstances,[30] in the 53 presidential elections since ratification of the Twelfth Amendment.

The Decennial Census Issue

An additional structural issue is that the electoral college system bases allocation of electoral votes on the results of each decennial census. After each census, all 435 Members of the House of Representatives are reapportioned among the states: some states gain Representatives, others lose them, and some remain unchanged. Gains or losses in House seats lead to comparable adjustments to state electoral vote allocations following the census. For instance, the most notable adjustments following the 2010 census were Texas, which gained four House seats and whose electoral vote allocation rose from 34 to 38, and New York, which lost two House seats, and whose electoral vote allocation fell from 31 to 29. The decennial reallocation of electoral votes is reflected in the first presidential election following the census; for instance, electoral college reallocations resulting from the 2010 census were in place for the 2012 election, and will continue for the 2016 and 2020 elections. This decennial reapportionment of electors fails, however, to account for significant population shifts that often occur *during* the course of a decade. Thus, the allocation of electoral votes for the next two elections will reflect the 2010 population distribution among the states, but makes no provision for changes during the decade. States that enjoy greater population gains during the current decade will not see those increases translated into more presidential electors until 2024. Until then, they will arguably be under-represented in the electoral college, while by the same logic, those that will ultimately lose seats and electors will be over-represented.[31]

The Faithless Elector

The Twelfth Amendment to the Constitution directs presidential electors to "meet in their respective States, and vote by ballot for President and Vice President, one of whom, at least, shall not be an inhabitant of the same state with themselves.... " It offers no further guidance beyond this instruction. There is ample evidence that the Founders intended electors to be representatives of their state political communities, free agents, able to vote for the persons they thought best fit for the presidency or vice presidency. Perhaps naively, they failed to anticipate the growth of partisanship and a nascent party system that emerged as early as President Washington's second Administration. The job of the elector was therefore quickly transformed from that of dispassionate judge to loyal party agent, expected to vote for the candidates designated by the party. So they remain today, and although nearly all electors since the earliest presidential elections have voted for the candidates to whom they were pledged, from time to time one or more electors have voted against the instructions of the electorate. Since the 1948 presidential election, nine "faithless" or "unfaithful" electors have cast votes for candidates other than those to whom they were pledged, and one cast a blank ballot.[32]

Twenty-six states and the District of Columbia attempt to bind their electors by one of several means, generally by requiring an oath or pledge or requiring electors to vote for the candidates of the political party the elector represents.[33] In 1952, the Supreme Court held in *Ray v. Blair* that political parties could exercise state-delegated authority to require elector-candidates for the office of elector to pledge to support the party's presidential and vice presidential nominees.[34] The Court did not, however, rule on the constitutionality of state laws that bind electors. Many commentators suggest that binding electors and the pledges that electors make are constitutionally unenforceable, and that electors remain free agents who may vote for any candidate they choose.[35]

From the standpoint of electoral college defenders, it may be noted that 9,137 electoral votes have been cast in the 17 presidential elections held since 1948. Of these, the eight that were indisputably cast against voters' instructions comprised less than one one-thousandth of one percent (0.00088%) of the total and had no effect on the outcome of any election.[36]

Legislative and Political Issues

The second category of asserted distortions caused by the electoral college arrangement stems from procedures that have been added to its constitutional provisions by the states over a long period of time. The most important issue is the nearly universal adoption of the general ticket, or winner-take-all, system for awarding electoral votes.

The General Ticket System—"Winner Take All"

The general ticket system of awarding electoral votes is cited by critics as a structural failing of the electoral college system, an issue that does not stem from the Constitution, but rather from state laws. At the present time, 48 states and the District of Columbia provide that the ticket of presidential and vice presidential candidates that wins the most popular votes wins all the electoral votes for that jurisdiction. By awarding all a state's electoral votes to the winner, regardless of the closeness of the popular vote results, the general ticket system is said to disenfranchise or discount the votes of citizens who preferred the candidates receiving fewer votes. This asserted inequity is said to be particularly apparent in states where the popular vote is closely divided.[37] Conversely, electoral college defenders claim the general ticket system's "multiplier" effect tends to reinforce the overall election results by magnifying the winning ticket's margin and deter frivolous challenges to the state-by-state results.[38]

Maine and Nebraska provide the only exceptions to the general ticket system, having established what is referred to as the "district system" of awarding electoral votes. In these states, as noted earlier in this report, votes are counted both by congressional district and on the statewide level. The candidates winning the most popular votes statewide are awarded the two electoral votes reflecting the state's "senatorial" electors, while the candidates winning in each congressional district are awarded one elector, reflecting the results in that district.[39] Proponents of direct election criticize the district system on the grounds that adding the "senatorial" electors to the statewide winners' total has much the same effect of disadvantaging the losing candidates and their supporters. District system supporters claim that it better reflects geographical differences in candidate support throughout a state, thus delivering an electoral vote that more accurately represents local preferences.

Alleged Biases of the Electoral College System

Opponents of the electoral college identify another category of alleged distortion built into the system. These are said to provide an advantage derived from state population or voter characteristics or behavior.

As the composition of the electoral college is partially based on state representation in Congress, some maintain it is inconsistent with the "one person, one vote" principle.[40] The Constitutional Convention agreed on a compromise plan whereby less populous states were assured of a minimum of three electoral votes, based on two Senators and one Representative, regardless of state population. Since electoral college delegations are equal to the combined total of each state's Senate and House delegation, its composition is arguably weighted in favor of the "small," or less populous, states. The two "senatorial" electors to which each state is entitled are said to confer on them an advantage over more populous states, because voters in the less populous ones cast more electoral votes per voter. For instance, in 2012, voters in Wyoming, the least populous state, cast 249,061 popular votes and three electoral votes for President, or one electoral vote for every 83,020 voters. By comparison, Californians cast 13,038,547 popular votes and 55 electoral votes, or one electoral vote for every 237,064 voters.[41] As a result of this distribution of electoral votes among the states, it is argued that "small" states have an advantage over large states because their electoral vote totals are larger in proportion to their population.[42]

While it is generally recognized that small states possess an *arithmetical* advantage in the electoral college, as noted above, some observers hold that, conversely, the most populous (large) states enjoy a *voting power* advantage, because they control the largest blocs of electoral votes. In combination with the general ticket system, this is said to confer an advantage on voters in these states because the large blocks of electoral votes controlled by the states have greater ability to influence the outcome of presidential elections. To use the previously cited example, a voter in Wyoming in 2012 could influence only three electoral votes, whereas a voter in California could influence 55 electoral votes in the same presidential election. According to this argument, known as the "voting power" theory, the electoral college system actually provides an *advantage* to the most populous states, and disadvantages all other states and the District of Columbia.[43]

Another theory centers on the asserted advantage enjoyed by ethnic minority voters. According to this argument, minority voters, principally African Americans, Latinos, and Jews, tend to be concentrated in populous states with large electoral college delegations. By virtue of this concentration, they are said to exert greater influence over the outcomes in such states because their voting patterns tend to favor candidates whose policies they perceive to be in their interest, thus helping win the states and their electoral votes for these candidates.[44]

A further alleged bias in the electoral college system is said to stem from the constitutional mandate that

> Representatives shall be apportioned among the several States according to their respective numbers, *counting the whole number of*

persons in each state (emphasis added), excluding Indians not taxed.[45]

Except for the two "senatorial electors,"[46] a state's electoral vote allocation depends on the number of Representatives in Congress apportioned to it. A state's electoral vote is based to this extent on residents, not on citizens, and therefore, it is asserted that states that have high numbers of noncitizen residents counted in the Census are said to enjoy a bias in the allocation of both Representatives and electoral votes.[47] For instance, the United States Election Project at George Mason University found that in 2012, 17.6% of California's population were noncitizens, the highest proportion of any state, followed by Nevada at 13.7 % and Texas at 13.5%.[48] A recent article discussing this asserted bias concluded that, due to large concentrations of noncitizens, California gained five electors from the most recent reapportionment, Texas gained two, and New York, Florida, and Washington each gained one elector that they would not have received if Representatives and electoral votes were allocated according to *citizen* population in the states, rather than their resident populations. Conversely, the author calculated that Indiana, Iowa, Louisiana, Michigan, Missouri, Montana, Ohio, Oklahoma, and Pennsylvania each lost one elector due to the noncitizen population advantage.[49]

Another alleged advantage or bias of the electoral college centers on voter participation in the states. Neal Peirce and Lawrence Longley, writing in *The People's President*, suggested that voters in states that have lower rates of participation may enjoy an advantage because it takes fewer popular votes per elector to win the state and all its electoral votes.[50] For instance, in the 2012 election, Hawaii, with four electoral votes, had the lowest rate of voter participation: 44.5% of eligible voters participated, casting 434,697 votes for President, a figure that equals 108,674 votes for each elector. By comparison, Minnesota, with 10 electoral votes, had the highest rate of participation, 75.7% of eligible voters, who cast 2,936,561 votes for president, a figure that equals had the highest 293,656 votes per elector.[51]

These various biases have been debated over the years. For instance, the alleged minority vote advantage was advanced by the Presidents of the American Jewish Congress and the National Urban League[52] as a reason for their support of the electoral college system during hearings before the Senate Judiciary Committee's Subcommittee on the Constitution as it considered a direct election amendment in 1979,[53] while Alexander Bickel also supported the electoral college in this context.[54] Conversely, other commentators have sought to refute many of the "biases" of the electoral college system.[55]

The "Electoral College Lock"

A final asserted bias considered in this report is the so-called "electoral college lock" that has been claimed to provide a lasting presidential election advantage to a particular party's candidates, originally Republicans, but more recently, Democrats. The lock is loosely defined as a tendency of the system to favor presidential candidates of one party over another. It is said to operate because a bloc of states possessing a large, sometimes decisive, number of electoral votes can be reliably expected to vote in successive elections for the candidates of the political party that tends to dominate those states. The lock is asserted to be dependent, as with other electoral college issues, on the general ticket system, which is examined earlier in this report.

In the late 1960s, political analyst and historian Kevin Philips developed a thesis that political and social developments were responsible for a political realignment that was arguably the most important factor in creating the lock. In *The Emerging Republican Majority*, he predicted that growing Republican Party conservatism and the Democratic Party's embrace of the civil rights movement and a socially and politically progressive or liberal agenda would combine with demographic developments favorable to the "Sunbelt" states to produce a restructuring of the nation's political balance in favor of the Republican Party.[56] Political commentators generally credit Horace Busby, a political advisor to President Lyndon B. Johnson, with naming rights for the lock.[57] During the 1980 presidential election campaign, Busby reviewed electoral college trends since the 1968 election and concluded that "... Democratic candidacies for the White House may no longer be viable. *The Republican lock* (emphasis added) is about to close; it will be hard for anyone to open ... between now and the year 2000."[58]

At the time Busby coined the term electoral college lock, the phenomenon was largely presumed to benefit the Republican Party. For a period of at least 20 years, beginning in 1968, observers pointed to a nearly uninterrupted string of GOP presidential election victories as proof of the lock.[59] Republican candidates won five of six elections during this period, taking an average of 417 of 538 electoral votes per election.[60]

In recent years, however, particularly since the 2008 and 2012 presidential elections, some observers have discerned a shift in the electoral college lock in favor of Democratic Party presidential candidates. They note that Democratic candidates have won four of the past six presidential elections by convincing electoral college margins, and that 18 states disposing of 242 electoral votes, sometimes referred to as "the blue wall,"[61] have voted Democratic in all six. This tendency is said to provide both a solid base for Democratic candidates, and a serious obstacle to Republicans in these contests.[62] It is attributed in part to the fact that social attitudes in the general public are said to have grown more favorable to Democratic candidates, and that, as one observer noted, "the demographic pendulum is swinging toward the Democrats. Young voters, Hispanics and a more active African-American electorate added states like Nevada, New Mexico, Colorado and Virginia to President Obama's winning coalition in the past two elections."[63] Since 1992, as noted above, Democratic candidates have won four of six presidential elections, taking an average of 327 electoral votes per election.[64]

Other observers, however, caution against accepting the electoral college lock as a deterministic given. They note that the purported locks of the 1960s through 80s, and that of the 1990s through the present can also be attributed to a wide range of factors, including such influences as domestic social and economic conditions, international issues of war and peace, U.S. involvement in conflict abroad, scandals of various sorts, candidate popularity, and even the competence, or lack thereof, of a presidential nominee's campaign.[65]

Electoral College Reform Options: End It? Mend It? Leave It Alone?

Congress may consider three basic options if it addresses the question of electoral college reform. The first choice, widely advocated for at least 50 years, would repeal the sections of the Constitution dealing with the electoral college—clause 2 of Article II, Section 1 and the Twelfth Amendment—and substitute direct popular election. The second, largely dormant for several decades, would reform the electoral college system by eliminating some of the alleged problem areas cited in the previous section of this report. A third option would be to leave arrangements as they are at present.

End It—Direct Popular Election Replaces the Electoral College

The direct election alternative would abolish the electoral college, substituting a single nationwide count of popular votes. The candidates winning a plurality of votes would be elected President and Vice President. Most direct election proposals would constitutionally mandate today's familiar joint tickets of presidential/vice presidential candidates, a feature that is already incorporated in state law.[66] Some would require simply that the candidates that gain the most popular votes be elected, while others would set a minimum threshold of votes necessary to win election—generally 40% of votes cast. Some proposals would require a majority to elect, and if no presidential ticket were to win either a majority or 40% of the popular vote, then the two tickets with the highest popular vote total would compete in a subsequent runoff election. Alternatively, some versions of the direct popular election plan would provide for Congress, meeting in joint session, to elect the President and Vice President if no ticket reached the 40% or majority threshold.

Direct Election—Discussion

Proponents of direct popular election cite a number of factors in support of the concept, many of which address the issues cited in the previous sections of this report. As their core argument, they assert that the process would be simple, national, and democratic. They maintain that direct popular election would provide for a single, democratic choice, allowing all the nation's voters to choose the President and Vice President directly, with no intermediaries. The "people's choice" would always be elected. According to supporters of direct election, every vote would carry the same weight in the election, no matter where in the nation it was cast. No state or group of voters would be advantaged, nor would any be disadvantaged. Direct election would eliminate the potential complications that could arise under the current system in the event of a presidential candidate's death between election day and the date on which electoral vote results are declared, since the winning candidates would become President-elect and Vice President-elect as soon as the popular returns were certified.[67] All mechanisms of the existing system, such as provisions in law for certifying the electoral vote in the states and the contingent election process, would be replaced by these comparatively simple requirements.

Critics of direct election and electoral college defenders seek to refute these arguments. Direct election proponents claim their plan is more democratic and provides for "majority rule," yet most direct election proposals require only a plurality—as little as 40% of the vote—in order to elect the President. Other versions include no minimum vote threshold at all, or provide for election by Congress in these circumstances. How, they might ask, are plurality Presidents or those elected by Congress, a practice they might note that was rejected by the Founders, to be reconciled with the ideal of strict majoritarianism? Opponents might further maintain that direct election would result in political fragmentation, as various elements of the political spectrum form competing parties, and regionalism, as numerous splinter candidates claiming to champion the particular interests of various parts of the country, entered presidential election contests. Further, they assert that direct election would foster acrimonious and protracted post-election struggles, rather than eliminate them. Under direct election, they suggest, every close election might resemble the bitter post-election contests in 2000, not just in one state, but nationwide, as both parties seek to gain every possible vote. They contend that such rancorous disputes could have profound negative effects on political comity in the nation, and might ultimately undermine public confidence in the legitimacy of the federal government.

Mend It—Reform the Electoral College

Reform measures that would retain the electoral college in some form have included several variants. Most versions of these plans share certain common elements. They would eliminate the office of presidential elector while retaining electoral votes; award electoral votes automatically, that is, directly to the candidates, without the action of electors; and retain the requirement that a majority of electoral votes is necessary to win the presidency. In common with direct election, most would also require joint tickets of presidential-vice presidential candidates, a practice currently provided by state law. The three most popular reform proposals include (1) the automatic plan, which would award electoral votes automatically on the current general ticket/winner-take-all basis in each state; (2) the district plan, as currently adopted in Maine and Nebraska, which would automatically award one electoral vote to the winning ticket in each congressional district in each state, but would also assign each state's two additional "senatorial" electoral votes to the statewide popular vote winners; and (3) the proportional plan, which would automatically award each state's electoral votes in proportion to the percentage of the popular vote gained by each ticket.[68]

Electoral College Reform—Discussion

Friends of the electoral college, as presently structured, or reformed, offer various arguments in its defense.[69] They reject the suggestion that it is undemocratic: electors are chosen by the voters in free elections, and have been in nearly all instances since the first half of the 19th century. They cite the electoral college as a major element in federalism, noting that the Constitution prescribes a federal election of the President by which votes are tallied in each state. As a federal republic, they assert the states have a legitimate role in many areas of governance, and that the Founders intended that in choosing the President voters act both as citizens of the United States, and as members of their state communities. Proponents of the electoral college maintain that the assignment of two electors to each state regardless of population is an additional "federal" component of the presidential election system, comparable to the two Senators assigned by the Constitution to each state. Further, they maintain the electoral college system promotes political stability. Parties and candidates must conduct ideologically broad-based campaigns throughout the nation in order to assemble a majority of electoral votes. The consequent need to forge national coalitions having a wide appeal has been a contributing factor in the moderation and stability of the two-party system. They find the "faithless elector" argument to be specious: as noted previously in this report, only nine electoral votes have been cast against instructions since 1820, and none has ever influenced the outcome of an election. Moreover, nearly all electoral college reform plans would remove even this slim possibility for mischief by eliminating the office of elector. On a practical level, they note that the general ticket system generally magnifies the winning ticket's electoral vote margin, an action they claim tends to bring closure to the election process and promote the legitimacy of the winning candidates.[70]

Supporters of direct election and critics of the electoral college counter that the existing system is cumbersome, potentially anti-democratic, and beyond saving. As noted earlier they maintain that the existing arrangement is the antithesis of their simple and democratic proposal. Its worst flaw has thwarted the public will on three occasions, by electing as President a candidate who received fewer popular votes than his primary opponent, and by throwing election into the House of Representatives in a fourth. They find the Twelfth Amendment's contingent election provisions to be even less democratic than the primary provisions of Article II, Section 1 of the Constitution.[71] They cite the decennial Census issue, the provision of "senatorial" electors regardless of state population, the prospect of the faithless elector, and the general ticket system as providing opportunities for political mischief and deliberate distortion of the voters' choice. They warn that although all states currently provide for choice of electors by popular vote, state legislatures still retain the constitutional option of taking this decision out of the voters' hands, and selecting electors by some other, less democratic means.[72] This option was discussed in Florida in 2000 during the post-election recounts,[73] and its survival demonstrates that even one of the more "democratic" features of the electoral college system is not guaranteed, and could be changed arbitrarily by politically motivated state legislators.

Leave It Alone

For nearly 30 years, the issue of electoral college held a prominent place on the agenda of successive Congresses. Between the late 1940s through 1979, hundreds of electoral college reform proposals were introduced in both chambers. They embraced a wide range of approaches to the question, but generally followed the outlines set out in the previous section: "ending it" by eliminating the entire electoral college system and establishing direct popular election, or "mending it" by reforming its more controversial provisions. The question of electoral college reform or replacement was actively considered throughout these years. Proposed amendments were the subject of hearings in the Senate and House Judiciary Committees on 17 different occasions between 1948 and 1979, and, most notably, electoral college reform proposals were debated in the full Senate on five occasions, and twice in the House during this period. Proposals were approved by the necessary two-thirds majority twice in the Senate and once in the House, but never in the same Congress.[74]

Following the 1979 defeat of a direct popular election amendment on the Senate floor, and the subsequent retirement or defeat of prominent congressional advocates, the question of electoral college reform largely disappeared from public attention and Congress's legislative agenda. The Senate's failed vote on a direct popular amendment marked the last occasion on which either chamber took floor action on an electoral college reform measure of any kind. With few exceptions, Congress has largely "left it alone" since that time. Although Senators and Representatives continue to introduce reform proposals in almost every Congress, few have received anything more than routine committee referral, and in time, the number of measures introduced per Congress has dropped almost to nil. Even after the presidential election of 2000, which featured a so-called "misfire," there was little evidence of support in Congress for constitutional reform of the electoral college system.[75] Since that closely contested election, the general ticket system's magnifier effect has generally conformed to contemporary expectations. In the presidential election of 2012, President Barack Obama and Vice President Joseph Biden, the Democratic nominees, were able to translate a popular vote margin of 3.85% (51.06% to 47.21%[76] and 65,899,660 popular votes to 60,932,152 popular votes) over Republican contenders Governor Mitt Romney and Representative Paul Ryan into an overwhelming electoral vote margin of 62.0% to 38.0% (332 electoral votes to 206).[77]

The most recently introduced constitutional reform measure was H.J.Res. 36, a proposed amendment that would have provided for direct popular election. Introduced in the 112th Congress by Representative Jesse L. Jackson, Jr., and 29 co-sponsors, the resolution provided that "the President and Vice President shall be elected jointly by the direct vote of the citizens of the United States, without regard to whether the citizens are residents of a State." This measure was referred to the House Judiciary Committee's Subcommittee on the Constitution, but received no further consideration.

No amendment proposing direct popular election or reform of the electoral college has been introduced to date in the 113th Congress, although H.J.Res. 7 would extend the right to vote for President and Vice President to residents of dependent territories and commonwealths of the United States.[78]

TRENDS IN CONGRESSIONAL ELECTORAL COLLEGE REFORM PROPOSALS

Within the context of declining congressional activity with respect to the electoral college, two trends emerge. First, the few proposed amendments introduced in the past decade all embraced the "end it" option, substituting direct popular election for the electoral college; no proposal to reform the electoral college has been introduced since the 107th Congress. Second, the scope of proposed direct popular election amendments arguably evolved in complexity and detail.

Given the contemporary context, it may be that the first development reflected a decline in electoral college support, lack of interest in reform proposals, or simply the absence of a sense of urgency. It is highly likely that supporters of the current system would coalesce to defend the electoral college if its existence or integrity were endangered. Recent actions by the Heritage Foundation and the State Government Leadership Foundation identified later in this report arguably confirm this thesis.

The second trend is that recent proposed amendments not only provided for direct popular election, but also included provisions to enhance and extend federal authority in such areas as residence standards, definition of citizenship, national voter registration, inclusion of U.S. territories and other associated jurisdictions in the presidential election process, establishment of an election day holiday, and ballot access standards for parties and candidates. If approved and ratified, provisions such as these would provide Congress with enhanced authority to establish broad national election standards, potentially superseding current state and political party practices and requirements, at least with respect to federal elections.[79]

The prospect of increased federal involvement in the administration of presidential elections raises two potential issues. The first is whether such federal involvement in traditionally state and local practices would impose additional responsibilities and uncompensated costs on state and local governments. If so, such requirements might be considered to be unfunded mandates, as they could impose additional costs on sub-federal governments, and as such would be subject to points of order on the floor of both the House and Senate.[80] One response by the affected state and local governments might be to call for federal funding to meet the increased expenses imposed by federal requirements. Precedent for this exists in the grant program incorporated in the Help American Vote Act of 2002 (HAVA).[81] An additional issue centers on perceptions that such an amendment and resultant legislation might be regarded as federal intrusion in state and local responsibilities. For instance, a far-reaching scenario could include the gradual assumption of the election administration structure by the federal government. In this hypothetical case, questions could be raised as to (1) the costs involved; (2) whether a national election administration system could efficiently manage all the varying nuances of state and local conditions; and (3) what would be the long-term implications for federalism. Conversely, it could be asserted that (1) a national or federal election administration structure is appropriate for national elections; (2) state or local concerns are counterbalanced by the urgent requirement that every citizen be enabled and encouraged to vote; and (3) every vote should be accurately counted.

STATE-BASED INITIATIVES SINCE 2004

While Congress has not acted on the question of electoral college reform in recent years, there has been considerable activity in the states. Only an amendment can alter constitutional structure of the electoral college, but the states retain considerable authority concerning various aspects of the system. For instance, as noted elsewhere in this report, Article II, Section 1, clause 2 gives the state legislature broad authority to "appoint" electors in any way they choose. In practice, this has been by popular election for 150 years. States also have authority over the formula by which electors are elected; as noted, 48 states and the District of Columbia use the general ticket system, but Maine and Nebraska adopted the district system or plan decades ago, an example of the states acting in their classic role as "laboratories of democracy." In other words, the states are free to experiment with systems of elector selection and electoral vote allocation, up to a point. Over the past decade, both proportional and congressional district plan proposals have been advanced in the states, as identified in the following section, but none has been successful to date.

California: District and Proportional System Proposals, 2008, 2012, and 2014

Since 2008, reform advocates in California have sought unsuccessfully to place legislative initiatives on the ballot that would have established the district plan on two separate occasions. In 2008 (the California Presidential Reform Act) and 2012 (the California Electoral College Reform Act), California district plan advocates proposed versions similar to those used in Maine and Nebraska as a legislative initiative to be decided by the voters. The 2008 initiative, in particular, was the subject of contentious political discussion and criticism on grounds that it violated the state constitution.[82] Supporters cited familiar arguments for the district plan, asserting that Republican votes in the Golden State were discounted by Democratic statewide majorities that took all 55 electoral votes in both elections. By comparison, if a district plan had been in place in California in 2012, the Democratic ticket, having won 41 congressional districts and the statewide vote, would have gained 43 electoral votes, whereas the Republican ticket, having taken 12 congressional districts, would have won 12 votes.[83]

In 2014, reform advocates proposed the California Split Electoral College Vote Distribution Initiative, which would have provided a rounded proportional allocation of electoral votes.[84] If the proportional plan as proposed had been in place in 2012, the Democratic ticket, with 60.2% of the popular vote, would have would have won 34 electoral votes; the Republican ticket, with 37.1% of the popular vote, would have won 20; and the Libertarian Party ticket, with 1.1% of the popular vote, would have gained one electoral vote.[85] Under the general ticket system, the Democratic candidates won all 55 electoral votes.

Ultimately, however, none of these proposed legislative initiatives reached the voters: supporters have been unable to gain enough petition signatures for any of the three to be placed on the ballot.[86]

Colorado: Proportional System Proposal, 2004

On November 2, 2004, Colorado voters rejected a state constitutional amendment, Amendment 36, that would have provided a rounded proportional allocation of electoral votes.[87] After a well-publicized campaign that gained a degree of national interest, the proposal was ultimately defeated by the voters.[88] Had the proportional plan proposed by Amendment 36 been in effect in Colorado for the 2012 presidential election, the Democratic Party ticket would have taken five Colorado electors with 51.5% of the popular vote, while the Republican ticket would have gained four electors from their 46.2% of the vote.[89] Under the winner-take-all system, the Democratic ticket received all nine Colorado electoral votes.

Michigan: District System Proposal, 2011

On November 29, 2011, a Michigan state representative introduced House Bill 5184, which proposed a standard district system for the election of presidential electors—one for winning the popular vote in each congressional district, and two for the ticket winning the statewide popular vote.[90] Advocates claimed the advantage for the district system that it makes every vote count, unlike the general ticket system, and better reflects geographical differences in candidate support within the state. Opponents claimed it was an effort to deprive the winning ticket of a majority of electoral votes in Michigan, citing in particular the 2012 presidential election results.[91] Under the proposed district system, in 2012, the Democratic ticket gained 54.21% of the statewide popular vote and all 17 Michigan electors. It won, however, only five congressional districts, so, under the District System, it would have gained seven electoral votes, one for each district and the two senatorial electors, while the Republican ticket, which won 44.71% of the statewide vote and nine congressional districts, would have gained a majority of nine electoral votes.[92]

Nebraska: Proposed Return to General Ticket System, 2013-2014

Nebraska established a district system for presidential elections in 1992, but only once, in 2008, has the state's five-elector delegation been split by party. Bills to return Nebraska to the general ticket or winner-take-all system have been introduced in the state's unicameral legislature several times in recent years. Proponents asserted that the district plan had weakened the state's influence in national politics, while opponents claimed that it actually promoted grassroots involvement in elections and public affairs, and that the split electoral vote in 2008 proved the validity of the district plan.[93] Some commentators, however, suggested that the proposed change reflected Republican concerns that the district system had energized Democratic voters in the 2008 election, leading to closer results than anticipated in the statewide presidential vote and other election contests that year.[94] One proposal, LB382, introduced on January 18, 2013, was the subject of hearings, but it was ultimately "bracketed" (indefinitely postponed) on April 5, 2014.[95]

Pennsylvania: District and Proportional System Proposals, 2011, 2013-2014

A district plan proposal introduced in the Pennsylvania legislature in 2011, and reintroduced in 2013, generated considerable publicity and political controversy. Senate Bill 1282 proposed to substitute the district system for the general ticket system used in the Keystone State since the earliest presidential elections. The bill proposed a standard district system, with one elector apportioned to each congressional district, and two at-large, representing the "senatorial" electors.[96] Supporters asserted that "[t]his proposal will more fairly align Pennsylvania's electoral college votes with the results of the popular vote. It will also make individual votes across the state more important, giving voters a more significant say in presidential elections."[97] Opponents, however, suggested the proposal was designed to break a 20-year Democratic hold on Pennsylvania's electoral college delegation.[98] In awarding electoral votes by congressional district, it was argued, Republicans might gain as many as 12 or 13 electoral votes from Republican-leaning districts under the district plan, even though the Democratic candidates won a statewide majority.[99] Opponents claimed the proposal was "a blatant power grab meant to rig presidential elections and diminish the voice of voters in Democratic strongholds."[100] Some Republicans also criticized the bill, on the grounds that the state Democratic Party organization might "move campaigns out of safe Democratic districts in urban population centers and into the more moderate suburbs."[101] SB 1282 was referred to the Committee on State Government on September 30, 2012, but no further action was taken during the 2012 legislative session. [102] An identical bill, HB 94, was introduced in the 2013-2014 session, but no action beyond committee referral had been taken by October 2014.[103] In the 2012 presidential election, the Democratic ticket won 51.97% of the Pennsylvania popular vote to the Republican ticket's 46.59% and all 20 electoral votes.[104] Had a district system allocation of electoral votes been in place in Pennsylvania in 2012, the Democratic ticket would have won seven electoral votes, having taken five congressional districts and the two senatorial electors awarded to the statewide popular vote winner, while the Republican ticket would have won 13 electoral votes, having taken 13 congressional districts.[105]

During the ensuing 2013-2014 legislative session, on February 21, 2013, 12 state Senators introduced Senate Bill SB 538, legislation that would establish a proportional system plan to award electoral votes in Pennsylvania.[106] This proposal differs from the classic proportional plan: it incorporates one of the district system's elements by awarding the two "senatorial" electors to the candidates who won the most popular votes statewide, but would award the balance on a rounded proportional basis. As with the earlier proposals, SB 538 aroused considerable media and press coverage and complaints by critics.[107] No action beyond committee referral has been taken on the bill at the time of this writing. Had this version of a proportional system been operative in Pennsylvania for the 2012 presidential election, the Democratic ticket, with 51.97% of the popular vote, would have won 12 electoral votes, while the Republican ticket, with 46.59%, would have won 8 electoral votes.[108]

Virginia: District System Proposal, 2012-2013

On December 3, 2012, a different version of the district system was introduced in the Virginia General Assembly as SB 723. In contrast to conventional district systems, which award each state's two senatorial electors to the presidential ticket *winning the most popular votes statewide*, this legislation would have awarded the senatorial electors to the presidential ticket that won the popular vote *in the greatest number of congressional districts statewide.*[109] As with similar recent state proposals, this bill proved to be controversial; supporters claimed it would more accurately reflect differing voter preferences by geographical regions, while opponents saw it "as an attempt to counter recent successes by Democrats." [110] The bill was "bypassed indefinitely" on January 29, 2013, by the Senate Committee on Privileges and Elections.[111] In the 2012 presidential election, the Democratic ticket gained 51.16% of the statewide popular vote to the Republican ticket's 47.28%, and won all 13 Virginia electors under the general ticket system.[112] If the district system variant as envisioned by SB 723 had been in effect for the 2012 election, the Democratic ticket, having won the popular vote in four congressional districts, would have gained four electoral votes, while the Republican ticket, having gained seven districts, would have gained one electoral vote for each district, and Virginia's two senatorial electors, for a total of nine electoral votes.

Wisconsin: District System Proposal, 2011

Shortly after Pennsylvania's SB 182 was introduced in 2011, the *Milwaukee Journal Sentinel* reported that district system legislation would soon be introduced in the Wisconsin state legislature. Arguments in favor of and opposed to the projected bill were similar to those raised in Pennsylvania.[113] Opponents, however, also claimed that the district plan would eliminate Wisconsin from the roster of "battleground" states. This, they asserted, would lead presidential campaign organizations and political parties to shift their resources to states where the winnertake-all system promised bigger electoral vote rewards for their campaign spending. Under this scenario, they claimed that the district system would ultimately cost the state economy millions of dollars in broadcast TV revenue, and even more from lost radio, cable, travel, staff, and other campaign-related spending.[114] At the time of this writing, however, no such bill had been introduced in the legislature.[115]

In addition to these specific plans, other states have been reported as considering changes to their current allocation of electoral votes in recent years, particularly Ohio and Florida. At the time of this writing, however, no measure has been introduced in the legislature of either state to this effect, and press accounts indicate that such actions are unlikely in the immediate future.[116]

NONGOVERNMENTAL PROPOSAL—NATIONAL POPULAR VOTE INITIATIVE (NPV)

National Popular Vote (NPV) is a nongovernmental initiative which seeks to establish direct popular election of the President and Vice President through an interstate compact, rather than by constitutional amendment.[117] Under the compact's provisions, legislatures of signatory states (including the District of Columbia) would appoint presidential electors committed to the presidential ticket *that gained the most votes nationwide*. Assuming all 50 states joined the NPV compact, this would deliver a unanimous electoral college decision for the candidates winning the most popular votes.

Northwestern University law professor Robert W. Bennett and constitutional law professors Akhil and Vikram Amar are generally credited as originators of the NPV concept.[118] NPV relies on the Constitution's broad grant (in Article II, Section 1, clause 1) of power to each state to "appoint, *in such Manner as the Legislature thereof may direct* [emphasis added], a Number of Electors, equal to the whole Number of Senators and Representatives to which the State may be entitled in the Congress."[119]

Specifically, the plan calls for an interstate compact in which the legislatures in each of the participating states agrees to appoint electors pledged to the candidates who won the *nationwide popular vote*. State election authorities would count and certify the popular vote in each state, which would be aggregated and certified nationwide as the "nationwide popular vote." The participating state legislatures would then choose the slate of electors pledged to the "nationwide popular vote winner," *notwithstanding the results within their particular state*.[120] Barring unforeseen circumstances, if all 50 states and the District of Columbia were to join the NPV, it would yield a unanimous electoral college vote of 538 electors for the winning candidates.

The compact, however, would take effect only if states controlling a majority of the electoral college, 270 or more votes, were to approve the plan. This would guarantee the plan's success by ensuring that at least 270 electoral votes would be cast for the candidates winning the most popular votes.

If the national popular vote were tied, the states would be released from their commitment under the compact, and would choose electors who represented the presidential ticket that gained the most votes in each particular state.

One novel NPV provision would enable the presidential candidate who won the national popular vote to fill any vacancies in the electoral college with electors of his or her own choice.

States would retain the right to withdraw from the compact, but if a state chose to withdraw within six months of the end of a presidential term, the withdrawal would not be effective until after the succeeding President and Vice President had been elected.

National Popular Vote, Inc.

The NPV advocacy effort is managed by National Popular Vote, Inc., a "501(c)(4)"[121] nonprofit corporation, established in California in 2006 by Barry Fadem, an attorney specializing in initiative and referendum law, and Stanford University professor John R. Koza.[122] As a 501(c)(4) entity, it may engage in unlimited lobbying and similar advocacy and educational activity so long as it furthers the organization's tax-exempt purpose and is not its primary activity. The primary activity restriction applies only to campaign activities.

NPV's board members include former Senators and Representatives of both major political parties, suggesting bipartisan support on the national level. As of September 2014, NPV claimed the support of 2,110 state legislators, over one sixth of the 7,382 total, and endorsements by the *New York Times*, *Los Angeles Times*, *Chicago Sun-Times*, *Minneapolis Star Tribune*, *Boston Globe*, *Miami Herald* and other newspapers.[123]

According to NPV, the compact has been introduced in the legislatures of all 50 states, and the Council of the District of Columbia. After initial momentum in 2008, when four states joined the compact in one year, NPV has made more gradual progress toward its goal of states disposing of 270 electoral votes. Previous highlights have been California's approval in 2011, which added 55 electoral votes to the tally, and most recently, New York's accession to the compact, finalized by Governor Andrew Cuomo on April 15, 2014. This action added the Empire State's 29 electoral votes to the total in states that have approved NPV, and brought it to 61% of its 270-vote operational threshold.[124] States that have adopted the NPV Compact, including their electoral vote allotments, are listed below, in chronological order.

- **Hawaii** (4 electoral votes), 2008;
- **Illinois** (20 electoral votes), 2008;
- **Maryland** (10 electoral votes), 2008;

- **New Jersey** (14 electoral votes), 2008;
- **Washington** (12 electoral votes), 2009;
- **Massachusetts** (11 electoral votes), 2010;
- **District of Columbia** (3 electoral votes), 2010;
- **Vermont** (3 electoral votes), 2011;
- **California** (55 electoral votes), 2011;
- **Rhode Island** (four electoral votes), 2013; and
- **New York** (29 electoral votes), 2014.

In addition to New York, the NPV compact was actively considered in six state legislatures in their 2014 sessions: Arizona;[125] Connecticut;[126] Minnesota;[127] Oklahoma, where it was approved in the Senate;[128] Michigan;[129]and Pennsylvania.[130] It remains to be seen whether New York's action will provide the impetus for further accessions in the near future; however, the legislatures in the first four cited states adjourned for the year without taking action, leaving only Michigan and Pennsylvania in session through the balance of 2014.

Conversely, proposals to rescind approval of the NPV Interstate Compact have been introduced in the legislatures of Hawaii, Maryland, Massachusetts, New Jersey, and Washington, to date, but none has been approved.[131]

NPV, Inc., claims bipartisan support, and includes a number of Republicans on its governing council; it may be noted, however, that all the jurisdictions that have joined the compact to date have been classified by a recent Gallup survey as "leaning" or "solid" in their support of the Democratic Party. For instance, 9 of the 11, including California, the District of Columbia, Hawaii, Illinois, Maryland, Massachusetts, New Jersey, Rhode Island, and Vermont were found by Gallup to be among the "most solidly Democratic states in 2013."[132]

Following California's accession to the NPV compact in 2011, various conservative or libertarian groups announced measures to defend the electoral college system. On December 7, 2011, the Heritage Foundation, a conservative public policy institute, hosted a forum at which guest speakers, including five state secretaries of state, expressed their concern over the National Popular Vote campaign.[133] On December 8 of the same year, *Roll Call* reported that the State Government Leadership Foundation, a project of the Republican State Leadership Committee, would begin a campaign to defend the electoral college and counter recent NPV gains.[134]

The National Popular Vote Initiative: Pro and Con

Arguments in support of and opposed to the National Popular Vote proposal resemble those for and against direct popular election; here again, the central issue turns on the question of the asserted simplicity, logic, and democratic attractiveness of the direct election idea as compared to a more complex array of factors cited by supporters of the electoral college system.

NPV—Pro

The National Popular Vote initiative is novel to the extent that it preserves the structure of the electoral college system, while guaranteeing that the ticket gaining more popular votes nationwide than any of its opponents would always be elected President and Vice President. At the core of their arguments, NPV supporters assert that the process would be simple, national, and democratic. Their core argument is that the compact "would guarantee the Presidency to the candidate who receives the most popular votes [or at least a plurality] in all 50 states (and the District of Columbia)."[135] It is also claimed to eliminate (1) the possibility of Presidents who won fewer votes than their opponent—there would never again be a presidential election "misfire" or another "wrong winner"; (2) faithless electors; (3) "disfranchisement" under the general ticket/winner-take-all system; (4) the various "voting power" advantages noted earlier in this report; and (5) the potential for contingent election under the Twelfth Amendment.[136]

Moreover, NPV advocates also assert the compact would provide a practical benefit to non-battleground "flyover" states. With "every vote equal," NPV maintains that presidential and vice presidential nominees and their organizations would need to spread their presence and resources more evenly as they campaigned for every vote nationwide, rather than concentrate on winning key "battleground" states.[137] For instance, according to *Every Vote Equal's* analysis of campaign appearances, the 2012 major party candidates for President and Vice President appeared at a total of 253 campaign events during the general election campaign, but they only visited 12 battleground states; 38 states and the District of Columbia were bypassed during the campaign.[138] NPV advocates also maintain that the concentration of campaign resources, advertising, and candidate appearances in battleground states depresses turnout in "flyover" states. NPV further suggests that this phenomenon may ultimately damage the ability to govern on the state and local levels and could have a negative impact on the legitimacy of public institutions.[139]

NPV—Con

Opponents may assert that NPV would undermine the Constitution and overturn the Founders' original intent. As noted earlier in this report, they could argue that presidential elections are not only national, but federal contests, in which the states have an important and legitimate role as envisioned by the Founders. The electoral college, they may assert, is an integral and important component of federalism, against which national popular election would be a serious blow. They might also argue that the National Popular Vote compact, despite its advocacy of majoritarian democracy, does not require that winning candidates gain a *majority* of the popular vote, but delivers the presidency to the ticket that gains *more* popular votes than any other.

Another criticism centers on what could be accurately defined as a fundamental change in the presidential election process and a *de facto* amendment to the Constitution. In fact, they could note, the NPV, as described by its founders, is an admitted "end run" around the Constitution,[140] circumventing the amendment process established by the Founders in Article V. One study opposing the plan asserted that because the use of an interstate compact "does not conform to the constitutional means of changing the original decisions of the framers, NPV could not be a legitimate innovation."[141]

Opponents might also assert that the NPV would eliminate the multiplier effect by which the electoral college tends to magnify the winning ticket's margin of victory, and confers a degree of added legitimacy to winners. NPV opponents could also argue that eliminating the multiplier effect would actually result in an increase in contested election results and legal challenges in the states, as the political parties maneuver to claim every possible vote.

Critics may also note that the National Popular Vote plan, launched in 2006, contains no "statute of limitations," unlike constitutional amendments, which must be approved by three-fourths of the states, typically within a seven-year period.[142] It may be noted that if NPV were a constitutional amendment proposed in 2006, it would have expired in 2013.

Finally, opponents might question the assertion that spreading campaign spending resources and candidate events in non-battleground states is a goal that justifies a profound change in the presidential election process. Candidate campaign appearances and spending, they might assert, should not be considered to be a local economic stimulus package; moreover, they might continue, it is equally dubious to assert that nominees will slight the concerns of citizens of the states from which they draw their greatest support, or that concentrated campaigning in the "battleground" states somehow "disenfranchises" voters in others.

National Popular Vote: Constitutional and Legal Issues

In addition to policy issues as discussed previously, some observers have also raised questions related to the National Popular Vote initiative based on the fact that it is an interstate compact as defined in the Constitution. Others have questioned whether NPV might interfere with some provisions of the Voting Rights Act. These issues are briefly identified below.

One issue turns on the status of the NPV initiative. NPV has been described by its supporters variously as a bill,[143] a state-level statute,[144] and an interstate compact,[145] and is generally considered to be the latter. An interstate compact is a contract agreement between two or more consenting states to establish an agency or authorize programs or functions that are carried out on an interstate basis.[146] Article I, Section 10, clause 3, requires that "No State shall, without the Consent of Congress ... enter into any Agreement or Compact with another State.... "

A related issue concerns the question of whether the National Popular Vote Initiative is an interstate compact that requires congressional consent. The National Popular Vote movement agrees that NPV is an interstate compact, but it maintains that the Constitution implicitly permits valid interstate agreements without the need for congressional approval on any subject that falls within the states' constitutional authority, as they assert the NPV compact would.[147]

Another issue is related to the Constitution's grant of authority in Article II, Section 1, clause 1, to the states to "appoint, in such manner as the Legislature thereof may direct," their electors for President and Vice President. The question has been raised as to whether NPV would violate the principles of federalism and deprive individual states of their influence under the electoral college.

One critic asserts the National Popular Vote compact might violate Section 2 of the Voting Rights Act (VRA) because moving from "a state-based [vote] to a national popular vote dilutes the voting strength of a given state's minority population by reducing its [voting power] ability to influence the outcome of presidential elections."[148] The same author asserts that the NPV compact may also violate Section 5 of the act.[149] In 2013, however, the U.S.

Supreme Court invalidated Section 4(b) of the VRA;[150] as a result, Section 5 has been rendered currently inoperable.

CONCLUSION

Barring unforeseen circumstances, the likelihood of major changes to the electoral college system by any of the three processes cited in this report—constitutional amendment, state legislation changing electoral vote formulae, or through the interstate compact proposed by the National Popular Vote campaign—appears to be low in the short term.

From the standpoint of a constitutional amendment, there has been little indication of congressional interest in this question during recent Congresses. The one relevant legislative proposal to date in the 113th Congress consists of an amendment to guarantee the right to vote in presidential elections by citizens who reside in U.S. territories.[151] Barring such unforeseen circumstances as an egregious electoral college "misfire," or some other highly contentious contest following the 2016 presidential election, there appears to be little impetus for congressional action in the immediate future.

The states may continue to consider legislative action providing for changes in their procedures for allocating electoral votes by either the district or proportional systems. To date, however, such proposals have generated intense controversy and opposition in the states where they have been introduced, being regularly characterized by opponents as efforts to rig presidential elections and deprive minorities of their voting rights. To date, none has been successful. Again, barring unforeseen circumstances, such experiments do not appear to enjoy widespread support, and even if enacted, they might be subject to legal challenges on various grounds, including dilution of minority voter influence.

Despite its successful adoption by California in 2011 and New York in 2014, the National Popular Vote interstate compact has yet to develop sustained momentum. While it has generated interest in various direct popular vote advocacy communities, it does not appear to have gained widespread awareness or support among the public at large. This could change, however, if NPV were to develop sustained momentum, or if more states were to join the compact, particularly populous ones like Pennsylvania (20 electoral votes) and Michigan (16 electoral votes), where the NPV compact was under active legislative consideration in 2014. Under these circumstances, proponents could be energized and encouraged by the apparent progress, while at the same time, opponents and supporters of the electoral college system might be expected to coalesce and mobilize around the issues identified in this report.

End Notes

[1] Direct election of the President is currently universal in presidential republics that provide for a strong chief executive, combining the roles of head of state and head of government, e.g., Mexico and Brazil. Presidents are generally indirectly elected in parliamentary republics, where the president typically has a ceremonial and non-political role as chief or head of state, while the prime minister, as head of government, exercises most of the executive authority associated with the presidency in the United States. Examples of parliamentary republics include Germany, Italy, and India. France combines aspects of both, providing for a powerful popularly elected president *and* a prime minister responsible to parliament.

[2] The unworkable formula required each elector to cast two votes for President, for different persons, at least one of whom could not be a resident of the same state as the elector. The candidate winning the most electoral votes, provided this constituted a majority of electors, was elected President, and the runner up was elected Vice President. This led in 1796 to the awkward result of "Federalist" John Adams being elected President as his political rival, "Jeffersonian Republican" Thomas Jefferson, was elected Vice President.

[3] Recall that George Washington was unopposed in the elections of 1788 and 1792.

[4] In 1800, Thomas Jefferson and his vice presidential candidate, Aaron Burr, reached a tie vote because the Jeffersonian Republicans failed to instruct one elector to cast a vote for someone other than Burr. The electoral college tie led to a bitterly contested contingent election in the House of Representatives.

[5] In 1824, no presidential candidate received a majority of electoral votes, so the House of Representatives elected the President by contingent election. In the election of 1836, no candidate for Vice President won a majority of electoral votes, leading to election of that officer by the Senate.

[6] The four exceptions are the presidential elections of 1824, 1876, 1888, and 2000.

[7] Clinton L. Rossiter, *1787 – The Grand Convention* (New York: Macmillan, 1966), pp. 198-220.

[8] 3 U.S.C. §4.

[9] U.S. Constitution, Article II, Section 1.

[10] Ibid., 23rd Amendment.

[11] Ibid., Article II, Section 1.

[12] Ibid.

[13] Neal Peirce and Lawrence Longley, *The People's President, The Electoral College in American History and the Direct Vote Alternative*, rev. ed. (New Haven, CT: Yale University Press, 1981), pp. 44-47.

[14] See U.S. Congress, Senate, *Nomination and Election of the President and Vice President of the United States, 2008*, "Part IV. State Laws Relating to the Nomination and Election of Presidential Electors," S. Doc. 111-15 (Washington: GPO, 2010), pp. 346-444.

[15] For more detailed information on the contingent election process, please consult CRS Report R40504, *Contingent Election of the President and Vice President by Congress: Perspectives and Contemporary Analysis*, by Thomas H. Neale.

[16] 3 U.S.C. §1, 62 Stat. 672.

[17] "Battleground" states are loosely defined as those 1) that possess large enough electoral vote delegations to have some influence on the election's outcome; and/or 2) are closely enough divided in party strength that a relatively small number of swing votes could deliver the state and its electoral votes to either candidate.

[18] For individual state requirements, see *Nomination and Election of the President and Vice President*, p. 380 for Maine, and p. 394 for Nebraska.

[19] 3 U.S.C. §7.

[20] U.S. Constitution, Article II, Section 1; 12th Amendment. The words "by ballot" are interpreted to mean by paper ballot. With respect to the location of meetings of the electors, the Founders reasoned that if they met in their respective states, there would be less opportunity for political intrigue and chicanery than if they assembled in a single location. The difficulties inherent in long-distance travel at the time may also have influenced the Constitutional Convention's decision.

[21] For further information, see Project Fairvote, "Faithless Electors," available online at http://archive.fairvote.org/ e_college/faithless.htm.

[22] 3 U.S.C. §15-18. The same sections of the U.S. Code provide for challenges to electoral votes, as occurred in 2001 and 2005.

[23] See, for example, Peirce and Longley, *The People's President*, pp. 2-9.

[24] Lydia Saad, "Americans Call for Term Limits, End to Electoral College," *The Gallup Poll*, January 18, 2013, at, http://www.gallup.com/poll/159881/americans-call-term-limits-end-electoral-college.aspx.

[25] See, for example, Martin Diamond, *The Electoral College and the American Idea of Democracy* (Washington: American Enterprise Institute, 1977).

[26] See, for instance, David W. Abbott and James P. Levine, *Wrong Winner, The Coming Debacle in the Electoral College* (New York, Praeger, 1991), Neal R. Peirce and Lawrence D. Longley, *The People's President, The Electoral College in American History and the Direct Vote Alternative* rev. ed. (New Haven, CT: Yale University Press, 1980), "Chances of a Misfire," pp. 116-119.

[27] In 1824, John Quincy Adams received fewer popular and electoral votes than Andrew Jackson, his major opponent, but was chosen President by contingent election, a process discussed in the next section of this report. In 1876, Republican Rutherford B. Hayes received fewer popular votes than his opponent, Democrat Samuel J. Tilden, but won a bitterly-contested election by one electoral vote. In the presidential election of 1888, Republican Benjamin Harrison received fewer popular votes than his major opponent, Democrat Grover Cleveland, but won the election with more electoral college votes. The incidence of a "minority President" occurred most recently in the closely contested presidential election of 2000, when Democratic candidates Al Gore, Jr. and Joseph Lieberman gained 50,992,335 popular votes to 50,455,156 for Republican candidates George W. Bush and Richard Cheney (*Congressional Quarterly's Guide to U.S. Elections*, 4th ed. (Washington: CQ Press, 2001), vol. 1, p. 688.) After a bitter dispute over election results in Florida that was ultimately decided by the Supreme Court, the Republican nominees were elected, having won 30 states with 271 electoral votes, while their Democratic opponents took 20 states and the District of Columbia with 266 electoral votes (one District of Columbia elector cast a blank ballot in protest against the outcome).

[28] For further information, please consult CRS Report R40504, *Contingent Election of the President and Vice President by Congress: Perspectives and Contemporary Analysis*, by Thomas H. Neale.

[29] There is evidence the Founders assumed that contingent election would become the norm, once the protean figure of George Washington passed from the scene. The assumption was that no subsequent candidate would be able to command the same level of nationwide recognition and support. See Peirce and Longley, *The People's President*, p. 26.

[30] Four closely matched major candidates contested the 1824 election, splitting the electoral vote.

[31] Abbott and Levine, *Wrong Winner*, pp. 82-83.

[32] In ascending chronological order they were: 1948: a Tennessee elector for Harry Truman (D), voted for Strom Thurmond (States' Rights); 1956: an Alabama elector for Adlai Stevenson (D) voted for Walter Jones, a local judge; 1960: an Oklahoma elector for Richard Nixon (R) voted for Harry F. Byrd; 1968: a North Carolina elector for Richard Nixon voted for George Wallace (American Independent); 1972: a Virginia elector for Richard Nixon (R) voted for John Hospers (Libertarian); 1976: a Washington elector for Gerald Ford (R) voted for Ronald Reagan; 1988: a West Virginia elector for Michael Dukakis voted for Lloyd Bensten (D), Dukakis's vice presidential running mate, for President; 2000: a District of Columbia elector for Al Gore cast a blank ballot; and 2004: a Minnesota elector for John Kerry (D) voted for John Edwards (D), Kerry's vice presidential running mate, for President.

[33] For individual state requirements, see *Nomination and Election of the President and Vice President*, pp. 310-345.

[34] 343 U.S. 214, 228-231 (1952).

[35] See *U.S. Constitution, Analysis and Interpretation, "The Constitution Annotated,"* Article II Analysis, Article II, Section 1, clauses 2-4, Election: Electors as Free Agents, available online to Members of Congress and staff at http://crs.gov/conan/default.aspx?mode=topic&doc=Article02.xml&t=1|4&s=1&c=2. See also Longley and Peirce, *The People's President,* pp. 96-101.

[36] Total and percentage computed by CRS. See also Peirce and Longley, *The People's President*, pp. 96-102.

[37] For example, in the 2012 presidential election, President Obama won Florida by a margin of 51.4% of the popular vote to Governor Romney's 49.1%. Under the general ticket system, however, the President also won all 29 of the state's electoral votes. Source: U.S. Federal Election Commission, *Official 2012 General Election Results*, at http://www.fec.gov/pubrec /fe2012/2012presgeresults.pdf.

[38] See also Peirce and Longley, *The People's President*, pp. 110-112.

[39] It should be recalled here and elsewhere in this report that despite the nearly universal reference to electoral votes as being awarded to the winning candidates, in fact, it is the tickets or slates of electors pledged to the candidates who win the most popular votes who are elected.

[40] The one person, one vote principle was established by the U.S. Supreme Court in congressional and state legislative reapportionment and redistricting, respectively in *Reynolds v. Sims,* 377 U.S. 533, 568 (1964), for state legislative districts, and *Wesberry v. Sanders,* 376 U.S. 1, 7-18 (1964), for U.S. House of Representatives districts, in order to insure equal representation for equal numbers of people.

[41] U.S. Federal Election Commission, *Official 2012 General Election Results.*

[42] Abbott and Levine, *Wrong Winner*, pp. 76-77; Gordon J. Hylton, "How Much Difference Does the Small State Advantage in the Electoral College Really Make?" *Marquette University Faculty Law School Blog*, March 8, 2010, available online at http://law.marquette.edu /facultyblog/2010/03/08/how-much-difference-does-the-small-stateadvantage-in-the-

electoral-college-really-make/. See also Peirce and Longley, *The People's President*, pp. 112-113.

[43] Peirce and Longley, *The People's President*, p. 125.

[44] See U.S. Congress, Senate, Committee on the Judiciary, Subcommittee on the Constitution, *Direct Election of the President and Vice President of the United States, hearings on S.J.Res. 28, 96th Cong.*, 1st sess., March 27, 30 April 3, 9, 1979 (Washington: GPO, 1979), pp. 163-219. The validity of these assertions was, however, questioned by Peirce and Longley in *The People's President*, pp. 127-130. Writing of conditions in the 1970s, they maintained that the electoral college system actually disadvantaged African American voters. For an opposing view, see Ronald D. Rotunda, "How the Electoral College Works, and Why It Works So Well," Cato Institute, Commentary, November 13, 2000, at http://www.cato.org/publications/commentary/how-electoral-college-works-why-it-works-well.

[45] U.S. Constitution, 14th Amendment, Section 2, clause 1.

[46] The two electors allocated to each state in addition to electors equal in number to its House of Representatives delegation are often referred to as "senatorial" or "constant two" because each state is assigned two, the same number as its Senate delegation.

[47] Leonard Steinhorn, "Without Voting, Non-Citizens Could Swing the Election for Obama," *Washington Post*, October 5, 2012, at http://www.washingtonpost.com/opinions/without-voting-

[48] George Mason University, United States Election Project, 2012 General Election Turnout Rates, at http://elections.gmu.edu/Turnout_2012G.html.

[49] Steinhorn, "Without Voting, Non-Citizens Could Swing the Election for Obama."

[50] Peirce and Longley, *The People's President*, pp. 113,114.

[51] George Mason University, United States Election Project, 2012 General Election Turnout Rates.

[52] U.S. Congress, Senate, Committee on the Judiciary, Subcommittee on the Constitution, *Direct Election of the President and Vice President of the United States*, hearings on S.J.Res. 28, 96th Cong., pp. 163-219.

[53] For further information on the alleged technical biases of the electoral college, see Lawrence D. Longley and James D. Dana, Jr., "The Biases of the Electoral College in the 1990s," *Polity*, vol. 25, no. 1, autumn, 1992, pp. 123-45 (the author of this report has been unable to identify any studies updating Professor Longley's work since his death in 2002); and U.S. Federal Election Commission, National Clearinghouse on Election Administration, *The Electoral College*, by William C. Kimberling, Washington, 1992, p. 12.

[54] Alexander M. Bickel, *Reform and Continuity: The Electoral College, the Convention, and the Party System* (New York: Harper and Row, 1971), pp. 4-9.

[55] See, for instance, Harvey Zeidenstein, *Direct Election of the President* (Lexington, MA: D.C. Heath, Lexington Books, 1973).

[56] See Kevin P. Phillips, *The Emerging Republican Majority* (New Rochelle, NY: Arlington House, 1969).

[57] Charlie Cook, "Color Them Competitive," *Cook Political Report*, January 30, 2007, at, http://cookpolitical.com/ story/1359.

[58] Godfrey Hodgson, *More Equal Than Others, America from Nixon to the New Century* (Princeton, NJ: The Century Foundation, 2004), p. 47.

[59] "Electoral College's Cold Calculus," *New York Times*, July 8, 1988, at, http://www.nytimes. com/1988/07/08/ opinion/the-electoral-college-s-cold-calculus.html.

[60] Statistics compiled by CRS from National Archives and Records Administration, U.S. Electoral College, "Historical Election Results," at http://www.archives.gov/federal-register/electoral-college/historical.html.

[61] David Gergen, "For GOP, a Scary 'Blue Wall' Awaits," CNN Opinion, November 4, 2014, at http://www.cnn.com/ 2014/11/03/opinion/gergen-blue-wall-republicans-2016/.

[62] Richard Baehr, "Electoral College: Advantage Democrats, American Thinker," March 1, 2013, at http://www.americanthinker.com/blog/2012/11/electoral_college_advantage_ democrats. html.

[63] Ron Brownstein, "The American Electorate Has Changed and There's No Turning Back," *Nationaljournal.com*, November 8, 2012 at http://www.nationaljournal.com/magazine/the-american-electorate-has-changed-and-there-s-noturning-back-20121108; "The Tarnish of the Electoral College," *New York Times*, November 15, 2012, at http://www.nytimes. com/2012/11/16/opinion/the-tarnish-of-the-electoral-college.html.

[64] "Historical Election Results," at http://www.archives.gov/federal-register/electoral-college/historical.html.

[65] Jonathan Bernstein, "The Electoral College: Not That Crucial," *Washingtonmonthly.com*, June 9, 2011, at http://www.washingtonmonthly.com/ten-miles-square/2011/06/the_electoral_ college_not_that030154.php; Mark Rhoads, "Democratic Electoral Lock is Nonsense," *Illinois Review*, February 26, 2011, at http://illinoisreview.typepad.com /illinois review/2013/02/dem-electoral-lock-is-nonsense.html.

[66] This provision, currently used in all states and the District of Columbia, requires each voter to cast a single vote for a joint ticket of two candidates, one for President and one for Vice President. This insures that the President and Vice President will always be of the same political party.

[67] For further information on the succession question, please consult CRS Report RS22992, *The President-Elect: Succession and Disability Issues During the Transition Period*, by Thomas H. Neale.

[68] For detailed information on the automatic, district, and proportional electoral college reform plans, please see CRS Report RL32611, *The Electoral College: How It Works in Contemporary Presidential Elections*, by Thomas H. Neale.

[69] See Martin Diamond, *The Electoral College and the American Idea of Democracy* (Washington: American Enterprise Institute, 1977); Tara Ross, *Enlightened Democracy, The Case for the Electoral College* (Dallas, TX: Colonial Press, 2004).

[70] Judith A. Best, *The Choice of the People? Debating the Electoral College* (Lanham, MD: Rowman and Littlefield, 1996) pp. 10-16.

[71] For more detailed information on the contingent election process, please consult CRS Report R40504, *Contingent Election of the President and Vice President by Congress: Perspectives and Contemporary Analysis*, by Thomas H. Neale.

[72] U.S. Constitution, Article II, Section 1, clause 2: "Each State shall appoint *in such Manner as the Legislature thereof may direct* [emphasis added], a number of Electors equal to the whole Number of Senators and Representatives to which the State may be entitled in the Congress.... "

[73] Michael White, "The Electoral College, A Message From the Dean," *Prologue* (National Archives), fall 2008, vol. 40, no. 3, at http://www.archives.gov/publications /prologue /2008/fall/electoral.html.

[74] For a detailed examination and analysis of these efforts, see Peirce and Longley, *The People's President,* rev. ed. pp. 131-206.

[75] Congress responded with the Help America Vote Act, enacted in 2002. For additional information, please consult CRS Report RS20898, *The Help America Vote Act and Election Administration: Overview and Issues*, by Kevin J. Coleman and Eric A. Fischer.

[76] The remaining 1.73% of the popular vote was cast for minor party candidates.

[77] U.S. Federal Election Commission, *Official 2012 Presidential General Election Results,* at http://www.fec.gov/ pubrec/fe2012/2012presgeresults.pdf.

[78] H.J.Res. 7, 113th Congress, introduced on January 3, 2103, by Delegates Donna M. Christensen, U.S. Virgin Islands, and Madeleine Bordallo, Guam. This proposal would authorize voting for President and Vice President by residents of "a territory or commonwealth of the United States." The resolution's relationship to the electoral college system is problematic, however, in that it does not seek to provide electoral votes for U.S. territories or the nation's other associated jurisdictions, e.g., American Samoa, Guam, the U.S. Virgin Islands, Puerto Rico and the Commonwealth of the Northern Marianas. If direct popular election supplanted the electoral college, this measure would arguably extend the right to vote for President to voters in these jurisdictions. The resolution was referred to the House Judiciary Committee's Subcommittee on the Constitution and Civil Justice. No further action has been taken to date.

[79] Congressional authority over federal elections stems from Article I Section 4, clause 1 of the Constitution for Congress, and Article II, Section 1, clause 4 for presidential electors. For further information and a detailed analysis of this authority, consult CRS Report RL30747, *Congressional Authority to Standardize National Election Procedures*, by Kenneth R. Thomas.

[80] For additional information, please consult CRS Report R40957, *Unfunded Mandates Reform Act: History, Impact, and Issues*, by Robert Jay Dilger and Richard S. Beth.

[81] Help America Vote Act (HAVA): P.L. 107-252; 116 Stat. 1666.

[82] Vikram David Amar, "The So-Called Presidential Reform Act: A Clear Abuse of California's Initiative Process," *FindLaw Legal News and Commentary*, August 17, 2007, available at http://writ.news.findlaw.com/amar/ 20070817.html.

[83] "Daily Kos Statewide Election Results by Congressional and Legislative Districts," *Daily Kos*, July 9, 2013, at http://www.dailykos.com/story/2013/07/09/1220127/-Daily-Kos-Elections-2012-election-

[84] Under a rounded proportional plan, percentages of the popular vote are rounded to whole numbers in determining the number of electoral votes awarded to competing candidates.

[85] Computed by CRS from California Secretary of State, *Statement of Vote, November 6, 2012 General Election*, at http://www.sos.ca.gov/elections/sov/2012-general/sov-complete.pdf.

[86] 2008: see Shane Goldmacher, "Electoral College Measure Falls Short," *Sacramento Bee Capitol Alert*, February 5, 2008, available at http://blogs. 2012: "California Electoral College Reform Act," *Ballotpedia, an Interactive Almanac of U.S. Politics*, at http://ballotpedia.org/ California_Electoral_College_Reform_Act_(2012). 2014: "California Split Electoral College Vote Distribution Initiative (2014), Ballotpedia, *an Interactive Almanac of U.S. Politics*, at http://ballotpedia.org/ California_Split_Electoral_College_ Vote_ Distribution_ Initiative_(2014).

[87] Amendment 36, available at http://www.lawanddemocracy.org/pdffiles/COamend36.pdf. Under the rounded proportional plan, percentages of the popular vote are rounded to whole numbers in determining the number of electoral votes awarded to competing candidates.

[88] Colorado, Secretary of State, *Official Publication of the Abstract of Votes Cast for the 2003 Coordinated[,] 2005 Primary[,] 2004 General [Elections]* (n.p., n.d.), pp. 138-139.

[89] The remaining 2.3% of popular votes were cast for candidates of other parties. Results computed by CRS from U.S. Congress, House, Clerk of the House of Representatives, *Statistics of the Presidential and Congressional Election of, November 6, 2012*, at http://clerk.house.gov/member_info/electionInfo/2012election.pdf.

[90] Michigan Legislative Web-site, 2011 session, House Bill5184, at http://www.legislature.mi.gov/(S(sknehimedm0y3k55mlybtnbu))/mileg.aspx?page= getobject&objectname=2011-HB-5184&query=on.

[91] Bryan Dickerson, "Don't Count on Snyder to Stop GOP's Electoral College Mischief," *Detroit Free Press*, January 12, 2014, at http://www.freep.com/article/20140 112/COL04 /301120077/electoral-college-Michigan-Rick-SnyderBarack-Obama-Mittt-Romney-popular-vote.

[92] FEC, "Official General Election Results for United States President, November 6, 2012," at http://www.fec.gov/ pubrec/fe2012/2012pres.pdf.

[93] "Electoral Vote Debate Begins," *Unicameral Update, the Nebraska Legislature's Official News Source,* January 29, 2014, at http://update.legislature.ne.gov/?p=14322.

[94] Don Walton, "Electoral Vote Change Stuck in Committee," *JournalStar.com*, *Lincoln Journal-Star*, March 10, 2011, available at http://journalstar.com/news/unicameral /article_6b78c3da-95fc-54c0-8f12-486e5e8a9fff.html.

[95] "Open States," at http://openstates.org/ne/bills/103/LB382/.

[96] SB 1282, Amending the Act of June 3, 1937, Regular Session 2011, Pennsylvania General Assembly web-site, available at http://www.legis.state 1282.

[97] "Senator Pileggi Unveils Proposal to More Fairly Allocate Electoral College Votes," statement, September 13, 2011, available at http://www.senatorpileggi.com/press /2011/0911/091311.htm.

[98] Pennsylvania voted for Democratic presidential candidates for every election since 1992.

[99] Aaron Blake, "Could Pennsylvania Republicans End the Electoral College as We Know It?" *Washington Post*, September 14, 2011, available at http://www.washingtonpost.com/blogs

[100] Dan Hirschhorn, "House GOP Fret Over Pa. Electorals [sic]," *Politico*, September 14, 2011, available at http://www.politico.com/news/stories/0911/63522.html. Here again, Professor Lawrence Longley's "voting power" theory comes into play. Substantial concentrations of Democratic voters, particularly minority voters, in the Philadelphia and Pittsburgh metropolitan areas have long been regarded as a key element in gaining a Democratic plurality or majority in the popular vote in Pennsylvania. A district plan system for awarding electoral votes would arguably lessen the voting power of minority votes in the state.

[101] "Pete Sessions: Pa. Electoral College Change Would Put House Races at Risk," *Wall Street Journal*, *Washington Wire*, September 15, 2011, available at http://blogs.

[102] SB 1282, Regular Session, 2011-2012, Pennsylvania General Assembly web-site, at http://www.legis.state.pa.us/ cfdocs/billinfo/billinfo.cfm?syear=2011&sind=0&body=S&type=B&BN=1282 .

[103] HB 94, Regular Session, 2013-2014, Pennsylvania General Assembly web-site, at http://www.legis.state.pa.us/ cfdocs/billinfo/bill_history.cfm?syear=2013&sind= 0&body= H&type=B&bn=94.

[104] U.S. Federal Election Commission, "Official General Election Results for United States President, November 6, 2012," at http://www.fec.gov/pubrec/fe2012/2012pres.pdf.

[105] Daily Kos Elections' presidential results by congressional district for the 2012 and 2008 elections," *Daily Kos*, at http://www.dailykos.com/story/2012/11/19/1163009/-Daily-Kos-

Elections-presidential-results-by-congressionaldistrict-for-the-2012-2008-elections?detail=hide.

[106] Senate Bill 538, Regular Session, 2013, Pennsylvania General Assembly web-site, at http://www.legis.state.pa.us/ CFDOCS/Legis/PN/Public/btCheck.cfm?txtType=HTM&sessYr=2013&sessInd=0&billBody=S&billTyp=B&billNbr= 0538&pn=0502

[107] "Bill to Change Electoral College System in PA Introduced," *Philadelphia Inquirer, "Philly.com,"* February 26, 2013, at http://www.philly.com/philly/blogs

[108] Computed by CRS from FEC, "Official 2012 Presidential General Election Results," at http://www.fec.gov/pubrec/ fe2012/2012presgeresults.pdf.

[109] Senate Bill SB 723, 2013 session, Virginia General Assembly, at http://lis.virginia.gov/cgi-bin/legp604.exe? 131+sum+SB723.

[110] Nia-Malika Henderson and Errin Haines, "Republicans in Virginia, Other States, Seeking Electoral College Changes," *Washington Post*, January 24, 2013, at http://www.washingtonpost.com/politics6654-11e2-85f5-a8a9228e55e7_story.html.

[111] Senate Bill SB 723, 2013 session, Virginia General Assembly, at http://lis.virginia.gov/cgi-bin/legp604.exe? 131+sum+SB723.

[112] U.S. Federal Election Commission, "Official General Election Results for United States President, November 6, 2012," at http://www.fec.gov/pubrec/fe2012/2012pres.pdf.

[113] Craig Gilbert, "Changing the Way the Electoral College Works in Wisconsin: A Recipe for Irrelevance?" *Milwaukee Journal Sentinel, Journal Interactive*, October 23, 2011. Available at http://www.jsonline.com/blogs 132415248.html .

[114] Ibid.

[115] Wisconsin Legislative Documents website, available at https://docs.legis.wisconsin.gov /2011/related/author_index/ assembly/A_LeMahieu_Daniel?view=section .

[116] Florida: Marc Caputo and Steve Bosquet, "Florida House Speaker Weatherford: Changing the Electoral College is for Sore Losers, *Miami Post Blog*, January 24, 2013, at http://miamiherald.typepad.com/nakedpolitics/2013/01/floridahouse-speaker-weatherford-rigging-the-electoral-college-is-for-sore-losers.html. Ohio: Kevin Robillard, "Ohio Skips Electoral Shift," *Politico*, January 29, 2013, at http://www.politico.com/story/2013/01/ohio-gop-skip-electoral-collegeshift-86882.html.

[117] For more detailed information and analysis of the National Popular Vote Initiative, please consult CRS Report R43823, *The National Popular Vote Initiative: Direct Election of the President by Interstate Compact*, by Thomas H. Neale and Andrew Nolan.

[118] Robert W. Bennett, "Popular Election of the President Without a Constitutional Amendment," *The Green Bag, An Entertaining Journal of Law*, 4 Green Bag 2d 241, available from the Social Science Research Network by subscription, see http://papers.ssrn.com /sol3/papers.cfm?abstract_id=261057; Akhil Reed Amar and Vikram David Amar, "How to Achieve Direct National Election of the President Without Amending the Constitution," *Findlaw's Writ*, December 28, 2001, available at http://writ.news.findlaw.com /amar/20011228.html.

[119] U.S. Constitution, Article II, Section 1, clause 2.

[120] Under NPV, assume that presidential ticket "A" won 55% of the popular vote in State "X," and ticket "B" won 45%. Under the current general ticket system, the state legislature would typically choose electors pledged to ticket A. Under NPV, assume the same in-state results, but assume that ticket "B" won the national popular vote. The state legislature, in compliance with the National Popular Vote compact, would vote to choose electors

committed to ticket "B," because that ticket won the national popular vote, notwithstanding the in-state returns.

[121] 26 U.S.C. 501 (c)(4). Non-profit tax-exempt organizations described in this provision of the Internal Revenue Code (IRC) may lobby for legislation and, so long as it is not their primary activity, participate in political campaigns and elections.

[122] Rick Lyman, "Innovator Devises Way Around Electoral College," *New York Times*, September 22, 2006, http://www.nytimes.com/2006/09/22/us/politics

[123] National Popular Vote website, available at http://www.nationalpopularvote.com/.

[124] Ibid., "Home," at "https://www.governor

[125] Arizona: in committee when the special legislative session adjourned May 29, 2014. National Conference of State Legislatures web-site, "2014 Legislative Session Calendar," at http://www.ncsl.org/research/about-state session-calendar-2014.aspx.

[126] Connecticut: passed in committee and pending when the legislative session adjourned May 9, 2014. Connecticut General Assembly web-site, at http://www.cga.ct.gov/asp /cgabillstatus/cgabillstatus.asp?selBillType=Bill&bill_num= HB05126&which_year=2014.

[127] Minnesota: tabled in the House, Minnesota State Legislature web-site, at https://www.revisor.mn.gov/bills/bill.php? b=House&f=HF0799&ssn=0&y=2013&ls=88; in committee in the Senate; legislature adjourned May 16, 2014 at https://www.revisor.mn.gov/bills/bill.php?f=SF585&y=2013&ssn=0&b=senate.

[128] Oklahoma: passed Senate, referred to House committee. Legislature adjourned May 30, 2014. Oklahoma State Legislature web-site, at http://www.oklegislature.gov /BillInfo.aspx?Bill=SB906&Session=1400.

[129] Michigan: active, in Senate committee; legislature normally remains in session through the end of the year. Michigan Legislature web-site, at http://www.legislature.mi.gov/ (S(kyesuf45i1k13rvtjsr1iuyb))/mileg.aspx?page=getObject&objectName=2013-SB-0291.

[130] Pennsylvania: referred to committee in House; legislature normally remains in session through the end of the year. Pennsylvania General Assembly web-site, at http://www.legis.state

[131] National Conference of State Legislatures web-site, at http://www.ncsl.org/research/elections-and-campaigns national-popular-vote.aspx.

[132] Lydia Saad, "Not As Many U.S. States Lean Democratic in 2013," Gallup Politics, January 29, 2014, at http://www.gallup.com/poll/167030/not-states

[133] Heritage Foundation, "The Electoral College and the National Popular Vote Plan," available at http://www.heritage.org/events/2011/12/electoral-college .

[134] Eliza Newlin Carney, "GOP Nonprofit Backs Electoral College," *Roll Call.com*, December 8, 2011, available at http://www.rollcall.com/issues. For further information on the State Government Leadership Foundation and its election-law-related activities, see the foundation's web-site at, http://www.sglf.org/election-law.

[135] National Popular Vote website, available at http://www.nationalpopularvote.com /pages/explanation.php.

[136] Contingent election takes place under the existing system if no candidates receive a majority of electoral votes. For further information, please consult CRS Report RL32695, *Election of the President and Vice President by Congress: Contingent Election*, by Thomas H. Neale.

[137] National Popular Vote web-site, available at http://www.nationalpopularvote/com /pages/explanation.php.

[138] Ibid.

[139] Koza, et al., *Every Vote Equal*, p. 38.

[140] This is the term applied by NPV founder, John Koza, in a 2006 interview: "When people complain that it's an end run," Dr. Koza said, "I just tell them, 'Hey, an end run is a legal

play in football.'" Rick Lyman, "Innovator Devises Way Around Electoral College." *New York Times*, September 22, 2006, available at http://www.nytimes.com/2006/09/22/us/politics/22electoral.html.

[141] John Samples, *A Critique of the National Popular Vote Plan for Electing the President*, Cato Institute, Policy Analysis No. 622, October 13, 2008, p. 9.

[142] Congress has set the seven-year period as a reasonable time limit for the ratification process for the 18th, 20th, and all succeeding amendments.

[143] "Explanation of the National Popular Vote Bill," National Popular Vote web-site, at http://www.nationalpopularvote.com/pages/explanation.php#exp_1page.

[144] "What Is the National Popular Vote Plan,?: Facts and FAQs," FairVote.org web-site, at http://www.fairvote.org/ reforms/national-popular-vote/what-is-the-national-popular-vote-plan/.

[145] "Explanation of the National Popular Vote Bill," National Popular Vote web-site, at http://www.nationalpopularvote.com/pages/explanation.php#exp_1page.

[146] Although compacts were originally used largely to settle boundary disputes among the states, in the 20th century they began to be used to address more complex, regional issues. At present, there are approximately 200 interstate compacts in effect, including such wide-ranging concerns as mental health treatment, law enforcement and crime control, education, driver licensing and enforcement, environmental conservation, energy, nuclear waste control, facilities operations, transportation, economic development, insurance regulation, placement of children and juveniles, disaster assistance, and pollution control.

[147] John R. Koza, Barry Fadem, et al. *Every Vote Equal: A State-Based Plan for Electing the President by National Popular Vote* (Los Altos, CA: National Popular Vote Press, 2006), pp. 284-285.

[148] David Gringer, "Why the National Popular Vote Plan is the Wrong Way to Abolish the Electoral College, *Columbia Law Review*, vol. 108, 2008, p. 208.

[149] 42 U.S.C. §1973c.

[150] 42 U.S.C. §1973b.

[151] H.J.Res. 7, introduced on January 3, 3013 by Delegates Christensen and Bordallo.

In: Proposals for Presidential Election Reform ISBN: 978-1-63482-933-5
Editor: Maureen Stone

Chapter 3

THE ELECTORAL COLLEGE: HOW IT WORKS IN CONTEMPORARY PRESIDENTIAL ELECTIONS*

Thomas H. Neale

SUMMARY

When Americans vote for President and Vice President, they are actually choosing presidential electors, known collectively as the electoral college. It is these officials who choose the President and Vice President of the United States. The complex elements comprising the electoral college system are responsible for one of the most important processes of the American political and constitutional system: election of the President and Vice President. A failure to elect, or worse, the choice of a chief executive whose legitimacy might be open to question, could precipitate a profound constitutional crisis that would require prompt, judicious, and well-informed action by Congress.

Article II, Section 1 of the Constitution, as amended in 1804 by the 12th Amendment, sets forth the requirements for election of the President and Vice President. It authorizes each state to appoint, by whatever means the legislature chooses, a number of electors equal to the combined total of its Senate and House of Representatives delegations, for a

---

* This is an edited, reformatted and augmented version of a Congressional Research Service publication, CRS Report for Congress RL32611, prepared for Members and Committees of Congress, from www.crs.gov, dated October 22, 2012.

contemporary total of 538, including three electors for the District of Columbia. Since the Civil War, the states have universally provided for popular election of the presidential electors. Anyone may serve as an elector, except Members of Congress and persons holding offices of "Trust or Profit" under the Constitution. In each presidential election year, the political parties and other groups that have secured a place on the ballot in each state nominate a "slate" or "ticket" of candidates for elector.

When voters cast a single vote for their favored candidates on general election day, Tuesday after the first Monday in November (November 6 in 2012), they are actually voting for the slate of electors pledged to those candidates. The entire slate of electors winning the most popular votes in the state is elected, a practice known as winner-take-all, or the general ticket system. Maine and Nebraska use an alternative method, the district plan, which awards two electors to the popular vote winners statewide, and one to the popular vote winners in each congressional district. Electors assemble in their respective states on the Monday after the second Wednesday in December (December 17 in 2012). They are expected to vote for the candidates they represent. Separate ballots are cast for President and Vice President, after which the electoral college ceases to exist until the next presidential election. State electoral vote results are reported to Congress and are counted and declared at a joint session of Congress, usually held on January 6 of the year succeeding the election, a date that may be altered by legislation. Since January 6 falls on a Sunday in 2013, Congress will likely set another date for the joint session in 2013, possibly January 8. A majority of electoral votes (currently 270 of 538) is required to win, but the results submitted by any state are open to challenge at the joint session, as provided by law.

Past proposals for change by constitutional amendment have included various reform options and direct popular election, which would eliminate the electoral college system, but no substantive action on this issue has been taken in Congress for more than 20 years. At present, however, a non-governmental organization, the National Popular Vote (NPV) campaign, proposes to reform the electoral college by action taken at the state level; eight states and the District of Columbia have approved the NPV compact to date.

INTRODUCTION

The President and Vice President of the United States are chosen indirectly by a group of persons elected by American voters. These officials are known as electors, and the institution is referred to collectively as the electoral college. The electoral college, and the system that has grown up around it, are criticized by some as an undemocratic anachronism, and praised by others as a pillar of political stability and the federal system. Absent a constitutional amendment, or the success of non-governmental "reform" initiatives, however, this system will continue to govern U.S. presidential elections for the foreseeable future. While the electoral college has delivered "the people's choice" in 47 of 51 elections since ratification of the 12th Amendment, it can and has delivered Presidents who received fewer popular votes than their major opponents. Moreover, in the highly charged political atmosphere of contemporary presidential elections, a tie vote in the college, the failure of any candidate to receive a majority of electoral votes, or an extremely close election—in either popular or electoral votes—could lead to an acrimonious and protracted political struggle, or even a constitutional crisis. Historically, since ratification of the 12th Amendment, the elections of 1824, 1876, and 1888 revealed the weaknesses of the system, and in the case of 1824 and 1876, arguably brought the nation to the brink of civil violence. More recently, the controversial presidential election of 2000, in which George W. Bush narrowly won the electoral vote and the presidency with fewer popular votes than his major opponent, Al Gore, Jr., continues to influence the tone and content of American political discourse more than a decade later. The potential for a similar or even more bitterly contested struggle in a future election argues for a reasonable level of familiarity with the various components and functions of this complex institution, which this report seeks to provide.

CONSTITUTIONAL ORIGINS

The Constitutional Convention of 1787 considered several methods of electing the President, including selection by Congress, by the governors of the states, by the state legislatures, by a special group of Members of Congress chosen by lot, and by direct popular election. Late in the convention, the matter was referred to the Committee of Eleven on Postponed Matters, which devised the electoral college system in its original form.[1] This plan, which met with widespread approval by the delegates, was incorporated into the final document with only minor changes. As devised by the committee, the electoral college met several standards; it sought to

- reconcile and balance differing state and federal interests;
- give the states, at their discretion, the authority to provide for popular participation in the election, or to retain control of the process within the legislature;
- by providing the "constant two" or "senatorial electors," afford the "smaller" states some additional leverage, so the election process would not be totally dominated by the more populous states;
- preserve the presidency as independent of Congress for election and reelection; and
- generally insulate the election process from political manipulation.

In the final analysis, the electoral college method of electing the President and Vice President was perhaps the best deal the delegates felt they could get—one of many compromises that contributed to the convention's success. Alexander Hamilton expressed the convention's satisfaction, and perhaps the delegates' relief at the solution they had crafted, when he wrote this of the electoral college in *The Federalist:*

> The mode of appointment of the Chief Magistrate of the United States is almost the only part of the system, of any consequence, which has escaped without severe censure, or which has received the slightest mark of approbation from its opponents.... I venture somewhat further, and hesitate not to affirm that if the manner of it be not perfect, it is at least excellent. It united in an eminent degree all the advantages the union of which was to be wished for.[2]

The Original Constitutional System

The Constitution gave each state a number of electors equal to the combined total of its Senate and House of Representatives membership.[3] The electors were to be chosen by the states "in such Manner as the Legislature thereof may direct" (Article II, Section 1). Qualifications for the office were broad: the only persons prohibited from serving as electors are Senators, Representatives, and persons "holding an Office of Trust or Profit under the United States."[4]

In order to forestall partisan intrigue and manipulation, the electors were required to assemble as separate groups in their respective states and cast their ballots as separate delegations in their respective states, rather than meet as a body in a single location.

At least one of the candidates for whom the electors voted was required to be an inhabitant of another state. This was intended to counter what the framers feared would be a provincial insularity once George Washington, the indispensable figure who, it was universally assumed, would be the first President, had left the political scene. By requiring one of the candidates to be from somewhere else, the convention delegates hoped to prod the electors to look beyond the borders of their own state or region in search of presidential timber.

A number of votes equal to a majority of the whole number of electors was necessary to elect. This requirement was intended to insure that the winning candidate enjoyed broad support, while election by the House of Representatives was provided as a default method in the event of electoral college deadlock. Finally, Congress was empowered to set nationwide dates for choice and meeting of electors.

The 12th Amendment Repairs Flaws in the Original System

The original method of electing the President and Vice President, however, proved unworkable. Under this system, each elector cast two votes for two different candidates for the office of *President*, but no votes for *Vice President*. The candidate who received the most electoral votes was elected, provided he received a number of votes equal to a majority of the whole number of *electors*—not a majority of *electoral votes*. Nobody actually ran for Vice President—the runner-up in the presidential contest was elected to the second office. This system, which was intended to bring the two best qualified candidates to office, never anticipated the early growth of political parties and factions, each of which offered a joint ticket of two candidates—one for President and one for Vice President.

By the third election, in 1796, the nascent political parties of the day, Federalists and anti-Federalists (also known as Jeffersonians or Republicans[5]), each offered a joint ticket. Under the original arrangement, the only way to make the system work was for all of the party's electors to cast one of their two votes for the recognized presidential candidate, and all *but one* of the electors cast their second votes for the vice presidential candidate. One elector would be instructed to withhold his second vote for the designated vice presidential candidate, so that the two candidates would not tie the vote and throw the election to the House.

This cumbersome system broke down almost immediately, in 1800, when a Republican elector failed to withhold his second vote from the acknowledged vice presidential candidate. This led to a tie between presidential candidate Thomas Jefferson and his running mate, Aaron Burr, leaving the election to be decided in the House of Representatives. The constitutional crisis resulting from the election of 1800 led to the 12th Amendment, which was proposed by Congress and speedily ratified by the states, as noted later in this report.[6]

THE ELECTORAL COLLEGE TODAY[7]

Notwithstanding the founders' efforts, the electoral college system almost never functioned as they intended, but, as with so many constitutional provisions, the document prescribed only the system's basic elements, leaving ample room for development. As the republic evolved, so did the electoral college system, and, by the late 19th century, the following range of constitutional, federal and state legal, and political elements of the contemporary system were in place.

Who Are the Electors?[8]

The Constitution, as noted earlier in this report, states what the electors *may not be*; that is, it prohibits Senators, Representatives, and persons holding an "Office of Trust or Profit under the United States" from serving. In effect, this language bars not only Members of the two houses of Congress, but any person who is an employee of the United States government—justices, judges, and staff of the U.S. courts and the federal judiciary; all political employees of the legislative and executive branches; federal professional civilian employees—"civil servants;" and U.S. military and law enforcement personnel.[9]

In practice, the two major political parties tend to nominate a mixture of well-known figures such as governors and other state and local elected officials, party activists, local and state celebrities, and "ordinary" citizens for the office of elector.

While they may be well-known persons, electors generally receive little recognition as such. In fact, in most states, the names of individual elector-candidates do not appear anywhere on the ballot; instead only those of the presidential and vice presidential candidates appear, sometimes prefaced by the words "electors for." Moreover, electoral votes are commonly referred to as having "been awarded" to the winning candidate, as if no human beings were involved in the process.

Nominating Elector-Candidates: Diverse State Procedures

The Constitution and federal law are silent on nomination procedures for elector-candidates, so the process of nominating elector-candidates is another of the many aspects of this system left to state and political party preferences. Most states prescribe one of two methods:

32 states and the District of Columbia provide by law that major party candidates for presidential elector be nominated by state party conventions, while five states provide by law for nomination by the state party's central committee. The remainder use a variety of methods, including unspecified party option, nomination by the governor (on recommendation of party committees), by primary election, and by the party's presidential nominee. Provisions governing new and minor political parties, as well as independent candidacies, are generally prescribed in state law, and are even more widely varied.[10]

How Are Electoral Votes Allocated Among the States?

The Constitution gives each state a number of electors equal to the combined total of its Senate membership (two for each state) and House of Representatives delegation (currently ranging from one to 53, depending on population). The 23rd Amendment provides an additional three electors to the District of Columbia.

The total number of electoral votes per state, based on the most recent (2010) census, ranges from three, for seven states and the District of Columbia, to 55 for California, the most populous state. *Figure A-1* and *Table A-1* in the appendix of this report provide current electoral vote allocations by state and D.C. for the elections of 2012, 2016, and 2020.

These totals are adjusted following each decennial census in a process called reapportionment, which reallocates the number of Members of the House of Representatives to reflect changing rates of population growth (or decline) among the states.[11] Thus, a state may gain or lose electors following reapportionment, as it gains or loses Representatives, but it always retains its two "senatorial" electors, and at least one more reflecting its House delegation. The current allocation among the states is in effect for the presidential elections of 2012, 2016, and 2020; electoral votes will next be reallocated following the 2020 census, an alignment that will be in effect for the 2024 and 2028 elections.

How Are the Electors Chosen?

The Constitution specifically grants the right to decide how electors will be *chosen*—as opposed to being *nominated*—to the legislatures of the several states:

> Each State shall appoint, in such Manner as the Legislature thereof may direct, a Number of Electors, equal to the whole Number of Senators and Representatives to which the State may be entitled in the Congress.[12]

Today, all presidential electors are chosen by the voters, but, in the early Republic, more than half the states chose electors by votes of the legislators in their legislatures, thus eliminating any direct involvement by the voting public in the election. This practice changed rapidly after the turn of the 19th century, however, as the right to vote was extended to an ever-wider segment of the population, culminating in the extension of the franchise to all eligible citizens 18 years of age or older. The tradition that the voters choose the presidential electors thus became a permanent feature of the electoral college system quite early in the history of the republic.[13]

While the vote for electors has devolved to individuals, the constitutional power of the state legislatures to decide how the electors will be chosen remains essentially unimpaired.[14] This was illustrated as recently as 2000. During the political struggle that followed that year's presidential election in Florida, it was suggested that the state's legislature might step in to appoint electors if local election authorities and state courts were unable to determine who had won its 25 electoral votes by the deadline required by federal law (this so-called "Safe Harbor" provision is examined later in this report). Although many commentators asserted that a return to selection of electors by the state legislature would be an unacceptable retreat from democratic practices, no serious arguments were raised against the constitutional right of the Florida legislature to do so.[15]

The Electors' Task: Ratifying the Voters' Choice

Presidential electors in contemporary elections are expected, and, in many cases pledged, to vote for the candidates of the party that nominated them. While there is considerable evidence that the founders assumed they would be independent, weighing the merits of competing presidential candidates, the electors have been regarded as agents of the public will since the first decade under the Constitution.[16] They are expected to vote for the candidates of the party that nominated them. "Faithless" electors provide an occasional exception to that accepted rule.

Disregarding the Voters' Choice: Faithless Electors

Notwithstanding the tradition that electors are bound to vote for the candidates of the party that nominated them, individual electors have sometimes broken their commitment, voting for a different candidate or candidates other than those to whom they were pledged; they are known as "faithless" or "unfaithful" electors. Although 24 states seek to prohibit faithless electors by a variety of methods, including pledges and the threat of fines or criminal action,[17] most constitutional scholars believe that once electors have been chosen, they remain constitutionally free agents, able to vote for any candidate who meets the requirements for President and Vice President.[18]

Faithless electors have been few in number (since the 20th century, one each in 1948, 1956, 1960, 1968, 1972, 1976, and 1988[19], one blank ballot cast in 2000,[20] and one in 2004[21]), and have never influenced the outcome of a presidential election.

General Election Ballots

General election ballots, which are regulated by state election laws and authorities, offer voters joint candidacies for President and Vice President for each political party or other group. That is, voters cast a single vote for electors pledged to the joint ticket of the presidential and vice presidential nominees of the party they represent. This practice conforms to the Constitution, which provides for only one set of electors, although the electors vote separately for President and Vice President. This practice also eliminates the possibility that voters could pick and choose among electors from different parties.

Most states do not print the names of individual elector-candidates on the general election ballot. The most common variants are for only the names and party identification of the presidential and vice presidential nominees to appear on the ballot, in some cases preceded by the phrase "Electors for." Some states further specify in law that a vote for these candidates is a vote for the elector-candidates of that party or other political group.[22]

Winner Take All: How the General Ticket System Awards the Electoral Vote in Most States

While the Constitution is silent on the exact procedure for awarding each state's electoral votes, 48 states and the District of Columbia currently use the "general ticket" or "winner-take-all" system. The sole exceptions to this practice, Maine and Nebraska, use the "district" system, which is examined later in this report. Under the general ticket system, each political party or group or independent candidacy that is eligible to be placed on the ballot nominates a group (also known as "ticket" or "slate") of candidates for the office of elector equal in number to the state's total number of electors. As noted previously, voters then cast a single vote for the presidential and vice presidential candidates of their choice; when they do so, they actually cast a vote for the entire ticket of electors *pledged* to the candidates of their choice. The ticket receiving the most votes statewide (a plurality is sufficient) is elected. These people become the electors for that state.

As an illustration, this is how the general ticket system works in a hypothetical state, "State A." Assume that State A currently has 10 electoral votes, reflecting its two Senators and eight Representatives. The two equally hypothetical major parties, "Party X" and "Party Y" each nominate 10 persons for the office of presidential elector, pledged to the presidential and vice presidential candidates of their party. Voters go to the polls and cast a single vote for the ticket of party electors of their choice, although as noted previously, only the names of the presidential and vice presidential candidates are likely to appear on the ballot. Party X's slate of elector-candidates receives 51% of the popular vote; Party Y's slate receives 49%. Notwithstanding the closeness of the results, all 10 of Party X's electors are chosen, and Party Y wins no electoral votes in the state. The Party X electors are pledged to their party's presidential and vice presidential candidates, and they normally vote to confirm the choice of the citizens who elected them (the exception, as noted previously, would be the infrequent faithless elector).

The general ticket system has been favored since the 19th century, as it tends to magnify the winning candidates' victory margin within states and across the nation, and generally guarantees a national electoral college majority for the winners. It has, however, been criticized on the grounds that it effectively negates the votes for the runners-up. Returning to State A, some critics suggest that it would be more equitable, given the state of the popular vote, if a number of electors supporting Party Y's candidate were chosen. Alternative methods of allocating electors are examined in a later section of this report, under ""Mend It" — Reforming the Electoral College."

General Election Day

Elections for all federal elected officials are held on the Tuesday after the first Monday in November in even-numbered years; presidential elections are held in every year divisible by four (November 6, for the 2012 presidential election). Congress selected this day in 1845;[23] previously, states held elections on different days between September and November, a practice that sometimes led to multiple voting across state lines, and other fraudulent practices. By mandating a single presidential election day, Congress sought to eliminate such irregularities.

Other factors also contributed to Congress's choice of a November election day. By tradition, November was chosen because the harvest was in, and farmers had some leisure time, and thus were able to take the time needed to vote. Tuesday was selected because it gave a full day's travel between Sunday, which was widely observed as a strict day of rest, and election day.[24] The choice of Tuesday after the first Monday also meant that election day would never fall on the first day of the month, which was generally the day on which local courts convened. This was intended to avoid congestion at the county seat. Finally, travel was also easier throughout the northern states during November, before winter had set in.

The Electors Convene

The 12th Amendment requires electors to meet "in their respective states." This provision was intended by the founders to deter "intrigue" and manipulation of the election by having the state electoral colleges meet simultaneously, but in separate locations. Congress by law sets the date on which the electors meet, which is currently the first Monday after the second Wednesday in December (December 17, 2012).[25] The same law set the "safe harbor" provision, whereby in cases of disputed state results, if the said state has provided a means of resolving disputes prior to election day, and if this means has been used to reach a decision as to the election result not less than six days before the date on which the electors are scheduled to meet, then that decision is final.[26] The electors almost always meet in the state capital, usually in the capitol building or state house itself. They vote "by ballot"—paper ballot [27]—separately for President and Vice President.

At least one of the candidates must be from another state, a provision retained from the original constitutional provisions; as noted earlier, it was intended by the founders to promote the selection of nationally renowned candidates, and to prevent the electors from selecting exclusively "native sons."

The results are then endorsed, and copies are sent to the following officials:

- the Vice President of the United States (in his capacity as President of the Senate);
- the state secretary of state or the comparable state officer;
- the Archivist of the United States; and
- the judge of the federal district court of the district in which the electors met.[28]

The electors then adjourn, and the electoral college ceases to exist until the next presidential election.

Congress Counts, Ascertains, and Declares the Vote

Aside from the presidential inauguration on January 20, the final step in the presidential election process is the counting, ascertainment, and declaration of the electoral votes in Congress.[29] The House of Representatives and the Senate meet in joint session in the House chamber on January 6 of the year following the presidential election. Since January 6 falls on a Sunday in 2013, it is anticipated that Congress will set a different date, possibly January 8, for the joint session.[30]

No debate is allowed in the joint session. The Vice President, who presides in his capacity as President of the Senate, opens the electoral vote certificates from each state, in alphabetical order. He then passes the certificates to four tellers (vote counters), two appointed by the House, and two by the Senate, who announce the results.

The votes are then counted, and the results are announced by the Vice President. The candidates receiving a majority of electoral votes, currently 270 of 538, are declared the winners by the Vice President, an action that constitutes "a sufficient declaration of the persons, if any, elected President and Vice President of the States."[31]

Objections to State Electoral Vote Returns

Objections may be offered to both individual electoral votes and state returns as a whole. Objections must be filed in writing, and be signed by one U.S. Senator and one Representative. If an objection is received in the joint session, and is determined to be valid, then the electoral vote count session is recessed. The Senate returns immediately to its chamber, and the two houses of Congress consider the objections separately. By law,[32] these sessions cannot last more than two hours, and no Member of either house may speak for more than five minutes. At the end of this period, the houses vote separately to agree or disagree with the objection. The Senate then returns to the House chamber, and the joint session reconvenes. The decisions of the two houses are announced. If both houses agree to the objection, then the electoral vote or votes in question are not counted. Otherwise, the vote or votes stand as submitted, and are counted as such.[33]

This process was most recently used following the 2004 presidential election. An objection was raised to the certificate of the electoral vote filed by the State of Ohio at the joint electoral count session held on January 6, 2005. It met the required standards, being submitted in writing, and bearing the signatures of one Representative and one Senator. The joint session was duly recessed, and the two houses of Congress reconvened separately to debate and vote on the objection, which they rejected. The certificate of electoral votes submitted by Ohio was accepted, and the vote was duly recorded.[34]

A Tie or Failure to Win a Majority in the Electoral College: Contingent Election by Congress

The 12th Amendment, as noted earlier in this report, requires that candidates receive a majority of electoral votes, at least 270 of the current total of 538, in order to be elected President or Vice President. In the event of a tie, or if no candidate receives a majority, then choice of the President and Vice President "defaults" to Congress in a procedure known as contingent election.[35] In a contingent election, the House of Representatives elects the President, choosing from among the *three* candidates who received the most electoral votes. The Senate elects the Vice President in a contingent election, choosing between the *two* candidates who received the largest number of electoral votes.

Perhaps the most notable feature of contingent election is that each state has the same vote, regardless of population. In the House, each state delegation casts a single vote for President, while in the vice presidential election, each Senator casts a single vote.

2012 Presidential Election: An Electoral College Timeline

May-August 2012 — State party organizations nominate a ticket of candidates for elector for President and Vice President in their states.

November 6, 2012 — General Election Day. Voters cast one ballot for the joint ticket of their preferred candidates for President and Vice President. These are actually votes for the electors committed to the candidates they represent. December 11, 2012 — The "Safe Harbor" deadline. As noted earlier, if, on or before election day, a state shall have provided by law for determination of controversies or contests over the electors and electoral votes, and if these procedures have been applied, and results have been determined on or before this date, these results shall be conclusive, and shall govern in the counting of the electoral votes. December 17, 2012 — The electoral college meets. State delegations of electors meet separately in their respective states at a place designated by the state legislature. In practice, the electors usually meet in the state capital, often in the state house or capitol building. The electors vote "by ballot" — paper ballot — for President and Vice President. Certificates of the results are then transmitted to the President of the U.S. Senate (one copy), the Archivist of the United States (two copies), the secretary of state or equivalent officer of the state in which the electors met (two copies), and the judge of the U.S. district court of the district in which the electors met (one copy). December 26, 2012 — Certificates must be delivered to the officers specified above not later than this date.

January 6, 2013 — On this date, or another date designated by Congress, the Senate and House of Representatives assemble in joint session to count the electoral votes. The announcement of the state of the vote is deemed sufficient declaration of the persons elected President and Vice president.

RED STATES, BLUE STATES, BATTLEGROUND STATES

For the general public, perhaps the most widespread contemporary electoral college imagery centers on the "Red State/Blue State" and "Battleground States" characterizations that have emerged in mass media in recent years.

"Red State/Blue State" in contemporary political language provides a heuristic for defining a state's political record and voting pattern. Although there are always exceptions to the rules, Red states are generally considered to be those expected to favor the Republican candidates, while blue states tend to vote Democratic. According to press accounts, the categorization of states as "Red" or "Blue" originated during the presidential election campaign of 2000. Although national television networks had favored red and blue for their election-night electronic maps of the states for at least 20 years, they had not previously associated particular colors with either party on a consistent basis from election to election.[36] NBC television journalist Tim Russert is generally credited with making the first nationwide reference to "red states" and "blue states," in remarks he made during an October 30, 2000, broadcast of "Meet the Press."[37] The phrase quickly gained currency, and has since become a standard verbal identifier for defining a state's political record and voting patterns. The red state/blue state label is also often used to identify a state's political history over the longer run: Texas, which has voted for Republican presidential candidates in every election since 1972, is generally typed as a red state, while California, which has voted Democratic in every presidential election since 1988, is considered to be a blue state. A more recent addition to the political spectrum is the "purple state,"[38] one which is closely contested by the competing parties; Ohio and Colorado have been characterized as purple states.[39] Purple status can also be used to identify a state whose voters may be trending away from previous voting patterns to support of a different party. For example, Virginia, which voted Democratic in the 2008 presidential election for the first time since 1964, has been characterized by some commentators as a red state that may be trending from red to purple.[40]

The terms "Battleground States" and "Swing States" are generally used to identify those in which the major parties are closely matched, and which are less predictable in their presidential choices from election to election. In all but the most lopsided presidential election campaigns, the electoral votes controlled by battleground states will provide the margin of victory for the winning candidates. Presidential campaign organizations, therefore, generally direct a high proportion of funds and resources to winning the vote in battleground states. Similarly, the candidates spend more time campaigning in these states than they would in states where they enjoy solid margins of support.[41] This concentration of resources in the battleground states has been criticized by opponents of the electoral college system as short-changing the great majority of states and voters in terms of campaign attention and candidate visits:

> In 2004 and 2008, candidates concentrated two-thirds of their visits and ad money in the post-convention campaign in just six closely divided "battleground" states—with 98% going to just 15 states. The net effect is that two-thirds of the states, and 200,000,000 of 300,000,000 Americans are ignored in presidential elections.[42]

Moreover, this concentrated attention does not apparently end with the election. Writing in *The Rise of the President's Permanent Campaign*, political scientist Brendan Doherty noted that recent Presidents have spent a disproportionate amount of time visiting identified battleground states during their first term of office.[43]

Alleged Biases and Advantages of the Electoral College System

Critics of the electoral college often point to what they characterize as "biases" in the system: inherent constitutional provisions or political arrangements that tend to favor various states or classes of voter in the presidential election process. During the 1960s and 1970s, several of these biases were identified and widely debated when electoral college reform proposals were actively considered by Congress. Three particular phenomena were identified: the arithmetic advantage enjoyed by less populous states, due to the allocation of two "senatorial" electors to all states regardless of population; the "voting power" advantage enjoyed by voters in populous states due to the leverage provided by the general ticket winner-take-all method; and an asserted advantage enjoyed by minority voters concentrated in the same populous states, whose voting patterns can shift results in these states therein, and thereby exert a greater influence on the election.

Small State Arithmetic Advantage

As the composition of the electoral college is based on state representation in Congress, some maintain it is inconsistent with the "one person, one vote" principle.[44] As noted earlier in this report, the Constitutional Convention of 1787 agreed on a compromise election plan whereby less populous states were assured of a minimum of three electoral votes, based on two Senators and one Representative, regardless of state population. Since state electoral college delegations are equal to the combined total of each state's Senate and House delegation, the composition of the electoral college thus appears to be weighted in favor of the small states.

The two "senatorial" electors and the one "representative" elector to which each state is entitled may confer an advantage on smaller states over more populous ones because voters in the smaller states, in effect, cast more electoral votes per voter.

For instance, in 2008, voters in Wyoming, the least populous state, cast 254,658 popular votes and three electoral votes for President, or one electoral vote for every 84,873 voters.

By comparison, Californians cast 13,561,900 popular votes and 55 electoral votes, or one electoral vote for every 246,580.[45] As a result of this distribution of electoral votes among the states, it is argued that "small" states have an advantage over large states with regard to electoral vote allocation relative to their populations.

Large State Voting Power Advantage

While it is generally recognized that small states possess an arithmetical advantage in the electoral college, some observers hold that, conversely, the most populous (large) states enjoy a "voting power" advantage, because they control the largest blocs of electoral votes. For example, voters in more populous states are better able to influence a larger bloc of electoral votes than those in less populous ones, because of the winner-take-all method of allocating electoral votes.

Thus, to use the previously cited examples, a voter in Wyoming in 2008 could influence only three electoral votes, 1.1% of the 270 needed to win the presidency, whereas a voter in California could influence 55 electoral votes, comprising 20.4% of the necessary majority of electoral votes in the same presidential election. According to this argument, known as the "voting power" theory, the electoral college system actually provides an *advantage* to the six most populous states (California, 55 electoral votes; Texas, 38, electoral votes; Florida and New York, 29 electoral votes; and Illinois and Pennsylvania, 20 electoral votes each) and disadvantages all other states and the District of Columbia.[46]

Large State Ethnic/Minority Voter Advantage

Another theory advanced during debate on electoral college reform in the 1960s and 1970s, centered on the asserted advantage enjoyed by ethnic minority voters, which combines their voting patterns and their tendency to be concentrated in more populous states. According to this argument, minority voters (e.g., African Americans, Latinos, and Jews) tend to reside and vote in populous states with large electoral college delegations. By virtue of this concentration, they are presumably able to exert greater influence over the outcomes in such states because their voting patterns tend strongly to favor candidates whose policies they perceive to be favorable to their interests, thus helping to gain these states and their electoral votes for the favored candidates. According to this theory, since these more populous states enjoy purported "voting power" advantages, the influence of minority and ethnic voters is still further magnified. These arguments were advanced by the Presidents of the American Jewish Congress and the National Urban League as reasons for their support of the electoral college system during hearings before the Senate Judiciary Committee's Subcommittee on the Constitution as it considered a direct election amendment in 1979.[47]

"Mend It" — Reforming the Electoral College

Two alternative methods for awarding electoral votes that pass the test of constitutionality have long been available to the states, the district and proportional plans. They have historically been promoted as avoiding the alleged failings of the general ticket system, and, according to their advocates, they have an added virtue in that they would not require a constitutional amendment. A third reform option, the automatic plan, would, however, require a constitutional amendment.

The District Plan

The district plan or system, as noted in the summary of this report, has been adopted by Maine and Nebraska. Under this arrangement, the voters in each state choose two electors on a statewide, at-large basis (representing the two "senatorial electors" allotted to each state regardless of population), and one elector in each congressional district.[48] Each voter still casts a single vote for President and Vice President, but the votes are counted twice: first on a statewide basis, where the two at-large elector-candidates who win the most votes (a plurality is sufficient) are both elected, and then again in each district, where the district elector-candidate who receives the most votes in each district (again, a plurality is sufficient) is elected.

This is how the district plan might work in State A, which, as noted earlier, is apportioned eight Representatives in Congress, and thus, when its two "senatorial" electors are added, has a 10- member electoral college delegation. Assume that Party X receives 51% of the statewide vote, and Party Y, 49%. Party X's candidates for the two statewide (or senatorial) elector offices are thus elected. Assume also that Party X receives a plurality or majority of the popular vote in five of State A's eight congressional districts, while Party Y wins in the other three districts. Under the District Plan, the "district" electoral votes would be similarly awarded, so that Party X would receive the five district votes, which when added to the senatorial electors, would total seven electors, while Party Y would receive the three electors that reflected its congressional district majorities.

The claimed advantage of the district plan is that it is said to more accurately reflect differences in support in various parts of a state, and does not necessarily "disenfranchise" voters who picked the losing ticket. For instance, a state that has one or more large cities whose residents tend to support one party, and a large rural or suburban population with differing political preferences and voting patterns, might well split its electoral vote under the district system. Opponents suggest that the district plan, with its division of electoral votes within states, would more frequently lead to deadlocked elections in which no candidate receives a majority of electoral votes.

Maine has never split its electoral vote during the time the district plan has been in place, but Nebraska did so for the first time in 2008.[49] The Cornhusker state split its district votes, awarding four electors to Republican candidates Senator John McCain and Alaska Governor Sarah Palin, who won two congressional districts and the statewide vote, and one to the Democratic nominees, Senators Barack Obama and Joseph Biden, who received the most popular votes in the state's Second Congressional District.[50]

For the record, had the district plan been in place nationwide for the 2008 presidential election, the electoral vote tally would have been different, but the results would have remained unchanged. Under the current plan, the Obama/Biden ticket won 52.9% of the popular vote and 365 electoral votes, 67.8% of the electoral vote total. McCain/Palin won 45.7% of the popular vote, and 173 electoral votes, 32.2% of the electoral vote total.[51] Under the district plan, Obama/Biden would have won 301 (55.9%) electoral votes to 237 (44.1%) for McCain/Palin.[52] As its proponents claim, the allocation of electoral votes under the district plan, at least in 2008, would have more closely approximated the percentage of the popular vote won by the two major party tickets.

The Proportional Plan

The other commonly proposed option is the proportional plan or system, which has never been adopted by a state, but was the subject of a proposed Colorado constitutional amendment that was rejected by that state's voters in the 2004 general election. The proportional plan allocates electors and electoral votes in direct proportion to the number of votes won by each ticket of candidates. Unlike the district plan, it does not account for geographical voting patterns within a state, but allocates electors on a purely statewide basis. Two variations exist: the *strict* proportional plan, that would allocate electoral votes to thousandths of electoral votes, that is, to the third decimal point, and the *rounded* proportional plan, that would use some method of rounding to allocate only whole electoral votes.

This is how the rounded proportional plan might operate in State A, with its 10 electoral votes. For this case, assume Party X receives 59.679% of the popular vote, and Party Y receives 40.321%. When these totals are rounded, Party X would be awarded six electors, and Party Y would gain four.[53]

Proponents of the proportional system argue that this is the fairest plan, since it most accurately reflects in its elector/electoral vote allocation the preferences of the voters, acting as a statewide political community. They also note that it would provide recognition for new-party or third-party candidates that achieve a substantial level of support in a state. Opponents suggest that because the proportional plan also splits a state's electoral votes among various candidates, it could, like the district plan, lead to deadlocked elections in which no candidate receives a majority of electoral votes nationwide.

For the record, had a rounded proportional plan been in place nationwide for the 2008 presidential election, the electoral vote tally would have been different, but the results would have remained unchanged. As noted earlier, under the current plan, the Obama/Biden ticket won 52.9% of the popular vote and 365 electoral votes, which comprises 67.8% of the electoral vote total. McCain/Palin won 45.7% of the popular vote, and 173 electoral votes, or 32.2% of the electoral vote total.[54] Under the rounded proportional plan, Obama/Biden would have won 288 electoral votes, 53.5% of the total, to 249 votes, 46.3% of the total, for McCain/Palin. One electoral vote, from California, would have been awarded to Peace and Freedom Party candidates Ralph Nader and Matt Gonzales.[55] As with district plan, the allocation of electoral votes under the Proportional Plan in 2008 would have more closely approximated the percentage of the popular vote won by the two major party tickets.

The Automatic Plan

The automatic plan or system comes closest to replicating the current "winner-take-all," or "general ticket" system by which the winning candidates in a state take all the state's electors and electoral votes. Most versions of this proposal also eliminate the office of presidential elector, and award electoral votes directly to candidates who won the most popular votes (generally, a plurality) in a particular state. Unlike the district and rounded proportional plans, however, the automatic plan would require a constitutional amendment, because it would abolish the office of presidential elector.

Supporters claim it preserves what they consider to be some of the advantages of the existing system: first, they assert, it would continue to deliver all of a state's electoral votes to the winning candidates, thus contributing to decisive results in presidential elections; they claim it would also help maintain an ideologically broad and stable two-party political system. Opponents maintain that it would continue to "disenfranchise" voters who picked the losing candidates by using the winner-take-all device, and that, in common with other proposed electoral college reforms, it would not guarantee that the candidates winning the most popular votes would always be elected.

Reform Through State or Non-Governmental Alternatives

Constitutional amendments that would revise electoral college procedures or eliminate the system altogether are routinely introduced in every Congress. The obstacles faced by would-be constitutional amendments are considerable, however: they requires two-thirds approval in both houses of Congress, and ratification by three-fourths of the states, usually within a period of seven years. Although there were a number of noteworthy attempts to reform the electoral college system or replace it with direct popular election in the three decades following 1949, there has been no floor action in Congress on any related proposals since 1979, and the most recent hearings were held in 1992. In recent years, measures to change the nation's presidential election system are increasingly likely to have originated on the state level, or be offered by nongovernmental organizations. These have included

- Colorado Amendment 36, a rounded proportional plan initiative that was rejected by the state's voters in 2004;
- the California Presidential Reform Act (California Counts), a district plan proposal that failed to win ballot access in that state in 2008; and
- National Popular Vote, Inc., a campaign organized by a non-governmental public interest organization to promote an interstate compact under which participating states would agree to award their electoral votes to the nationwide popular vote winner.[56]

"End It" — Replacing the Electoral College with Direct Popular Election

The most widely introduced proposal to reform the presidential election system would scrap the electoral college altogether and replace it with direct popular election of the President and Vice President. Most direct election proposals provide that the joint ticket of candidates for President and Vice President that wins the most popular vote — a plurality would be sufficient — would be elected. Some versions of direct popular election would require candidates to gain at least 40% of the vote in order to win; generally these proposals would provide for a runoff election or election by Congress if the necessary percentage is not gained.

Proponents of direct popular election argue that it is simple, democratic, and foolproof: the candidates with the most popular votes would win under any conceivable circumstance.[57] Opponents, and defenders of the electoral college, claim that the existing system is an integral and vital element in the U.S. federal system, that it contributes to a stable and ideologically diverse two party system, and that it has delivered the "people's choice"[58] in 47 of 51 presidential elections since the 12th Amendment came into effect in 1804—what they characterize as an excellent track record.[59]

Concluding Observations

The electoral college system has demonstrated both durability and adaptability during more than two centuries of government under the U.S. Constitution. Although its constitutional elements have remained largely unchanged since ratification of the 12th Amendment, the electoral college has never worked quite the way the founders anticipated: as an indirect, deliberate selection process, carefully filtered from political considerations. Instead, it accommodated the demands of an increasingly democratic and political-party dominated presidential election system, ultimately evolving into a patchwork assemblage of constitutional provisions, state laws, political party practices, and enduring traditions that, with several notable exceptions, has delivered the popular vote winners in most presidential elections. Given the high hurdles faced by proposed constitutional amendments, it seems likely to remain in place unless or until its alleged failings become so compelling that large concurrent majorities in the public, Congress, and the states, are prepared to undertake its reform or abolition. In recent years, potential alternatives to constitutional change have emerged on the state level, and even in non-governmental advocacy campaigns, and it is arguable that these state and "grass roots" movements may have greater chances for success than a constitutional amendment. As noted earlier in this report, Colorado's Amendment 36 initiative was rejected at the polls in 2004, and the politically controversial "California Counts" initiative proposal failed to attain ballot access in the latter state in 2008. It is arguable, however, that the interest generated by such efforts may stimulate further experimentation in alternative electoral college plans, in which the states might serve in their classic role as "laboratories" for national policy. Moreover, the most notably successful electoral college reform effort in recent decades has been both non-federal and, in its origins, non-governmental. The National Popular Vote campaign, cited earlier in this report, has enjoyed a degree of success, having been approved in eight states (and the District of Columbia) that collectively control 132 electoral votes.[60] It has also been passed by one or both legislative chambers, but not gained final approval, in a number of additional states. Here again, however, the ultimate fate of the electoral college system arguably rests on the results it produces: in modern times, the college is expected to ratify the public choice by delivering the presidency to the candidates who have gained the most popular votes. If the electoral college system meets expectations, these proposals may languish. If it does not, they or others like them could attract sufficient popular and political support to become viable alternatives.

APPENDIX. ELECTORAL VOTE ALLOCATION BY STATES AND THE DISTRICT OF COLUMBIA

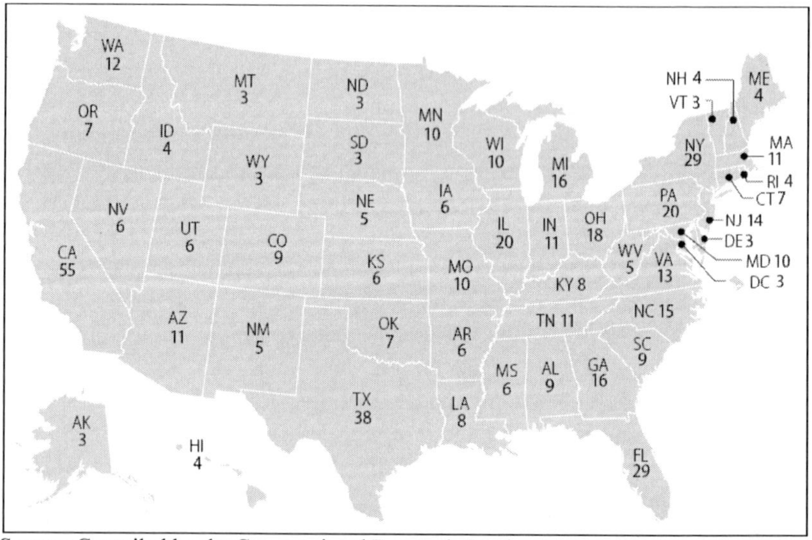

Source: Compiled by the Congressional Research Service.

Figure A-1. Map of State Electoral Vote Allocations, Presidential Elections of 2012, 2016, and 2020.

Table A-1. Electoral Vote Allocation by States and the District of Columbia, Presidential Elections of 2012, 2016, and 2020

State	Electors	State	Electors	State	Electors
Alabama	9	Kentucky	8	North Dakota	3
Alaska	3	Louisiana	8	Ohio	18
Arizona	11	Maine	4	Oklahoma	7
Arkansas	6	Maryland	10	Oregon	7
California	55	Massachusetts	11	Pennsylvania	20
Colorado	9	Michigan	16	Rhode Island	4
Connecticut	7	Minnesota	10	South Carolina	9
Delaware	3	Mississippi	6	South Dakota	3
District of Columbia	3	Missouri	10	Tennessee	11
Florida	29	Montana	3	Texas	38
Georgia	16	Nebraska	5	Utah	6
Hawaii	4	Nevada	6	Vermont	3
Idaho	4	New Hampshire	4	Virginia	13
Illinois	20	New Jersey	14	Washington	12
Indiana	11	New Mexico	5	West Virginia	5
Iowa	6	New York	29	Wisconsin	10
Kansas	6	North Carolina	15	Wyoming	3

Source: Compiled by the Congressional Research Service.

End Notes

[1] Although the term is not found in the Constitution, the electors have been known collectively as the electoral college since the early days of the republic, an expression that may be misleading, since the college has no continuing existence, never meets in plenary session, and ceases to exist immediately after the electors have performed their function.

[2] Alexander Hamilton, "The Method of Electing the President," in The Federalist, number 68 (Cambridge, MA: Belknap Press of Harvard U. Press, 1966), p. 440.

[3] A map and table portraying the current allocation of electoral votes among the states may be found in the Appendix to this report, on pages 19-21.

[4] U.S. Constitution, Article II, Section 1, clause 2.

[5] To avoid confusion, it should be noted that the "Jeffersonian" or "Republican" proto-party of the 1790s was the ancestor of the modern Democratic Party. The modern Republican Party, which also claimed descent from the Jeffersonians, emerged in the 1850s.

[6] For further information on the election of 1800 and the 12th Amendment, consult Neal R. Peirce and Lawrence D. Longley, The People's President, The Electoral College in American History and the Direct Vote Alternative, revised edition (New Haven, CT: Yale University Press, 1981), pp.36-44.

[7] For information on proposals to reform the electoral college, see CRS Report R42139, Contemporary Developments in Presidential Elections, by Kevin J. Coleman, R. Sam Garrett, and Thomas H. Neale; and CRS Report R42139, Contemporary Developments in Presidential Elections, by Kevin J. Coleman, R. Sam Garrett, and Thomas H. Neale.

[8] For a list of electors in the presidential election of 2008, consult the National Archives and Records Administration's website at http://www.archives.gov/federal-register/electoral-college/2008-certificates/.

[9] It is unclear whether the constitutional prohibition covers persons who serve without compensation on federal executive or congressional advisory boards and commissions. A 2007 opinion for the General Counsel of the Federal Bureau of Investigation (FBI) held that members of the FBI Director's Advisory Board should not be considered to hold an "Office Profit or Trust" under the United States, as described in the Constitution's so-called emoluments clause (Article I, Section 9, clause 8). From this opinion, it could be inferred that members of the said boards and commissions would not be covered by the Article II, Section 1, clause 2 prohibiting persons holding "an Office of Trust or Prophet" from serving as presidential electors. For further information, consult "Application of the Emoluments Clause to a Member of the Federal Bureau of Investigation Director's Advisory Board," Memorandum Opinion for the General Counsel, Federal Bureau of Investigation, June 15, 2007. Available to Members of Congress and their staff from the author of this report.

[10] For information on elector-nomination procedures in the individual states, please consult: U.S. Congress, Nomination and Election of the President and Vice President of the United States, 2008, 111th Congress 2nd sess., S. Doc. 111-15 (Washington: GPO, 2010), pp. 346-428. This is the most recent edition available in 2012.

[11] For additional information on the apportionment process, please consult CRS Report R41357, The U.S. House of Representatives Apportionment Formula in Theory and Practice, by Royce Crocker.

[12] U.S. Constitution, Article II, Section 1, clause 2.

[13] Peirce and Longley, The People's President, revised edition, pp. 44-47.

[14] The legislature's power is, however, subject to certain constitutional constraints, particularly if state procedures are found to have violated the equal protection clause of the 14th Amendment. For additional information, please consult U.S. Congress, Senate, The Constitution of the United States, Analysis and Interpretation, "Article II, Section 1, clauses 2-4," 108th Cong., 2nd sess., Sen. Doc. 108-17 (Washington: GPO, 2004), pp. 450-452. Also available online at http://www.gpo.gov/fdsys/search/pagedetails.action? granuleId =GPO-CONAN-2002-8-3&packageId=GPO-CONAN2002&fromBrowse=true.

[15] "Florida Legislative Leaders Call Special Session for Friday," CNN Politics, December 6, 2000, CNN.com, December 11, 2000, available at http://articles.cnn.com/2000-12-06/politics/fla.legislature_1_special-session-senatepresident-john-mckay-electoral-votes?_s=PM:ALLPOLITICS; and Jim Saunders and Randolph Pendleton, "Legislators Poised to Pick Bush Electors," Florida Times Union/Jacksonville.com, December 12, 2000, available at http://jacksonville.com/tu-online/stories/121200/met_4857971.html; and John C. Fortier, ed., After the People Vote, A Guide to the Electoral College, third edition, (Washington: AEI Press, 2005), p. 45.

[16] Peirce and Longley, The People's President, revised edition, pp. 24, 96-101.

[17] For information on these restrictions, please consult: U.S. Congress, Nomination and Election of the President and Vice President of the United States, 2008, pp. 346-428. This is the most recent edition available in 2012.

[18] U.S. Congress, Senate, The Constitution of the United States of America, Analysis and Interpretation, pp. 453-455. Also available in PDF format at http: http://www.gpo.gov/fdsys/pkg/GPO-CONAN-2002/pdf/GPO-CONAN-2002-8- 3.pdf.

[19] For the names of faithless electors and the circumstances under which they cast their votes, see http://archive.fairvote.org/e_college/faithless.htm.

[20] For the name of the elector and the circumstances under which this elector cast a blank electoral vote ballot in 2000, see http://archive.fairvote.org/e_college/faithless.htm.

[21] In 2004, one Minnesota elector cast votes for John Edwards for both President and Vice President. No objection was raised in the January 6, 2005, joint session at which electoral votes were counted, and the vote was recorded as cast. See National Archives and Records Administration website at http://www.archives.gov/federal-register/electoralcollege/scores2.html#2004.

[22] For information on individual state ballot format, please consult: U.S. Congress, Nomination and Election of the President and Vice President of the United States, 2008, pp. 346-428. This is the most recent edition available in 2012.

[23] Statutes at Large, 5 Stat. 721.

[24] In most rural areas, the only polling place was at the county seat, frequently a full day's journey for voters from the further reaches of a county.

[25] 3 U.S.C. 7.

[26] This requirement, found at 3 U.S.C. (5), was crucial in decisive allocation of Florida's electors in the 2000 presidential election.

[27] 12th Amendment. This provision has historically been interpreted to require paper ballots for President and Vice President.

[28] 3 U.S.C. 11.

[29] 3 U.S.C. 15-18.

[30] This action is usually accomplished by a joint resolution originating in the House. For the 2009 joint session, for instance, the date was set by H.J.Res. 100, 110th Congress. At the time of this writing, no resolution concerning the date for the joint session has been introduced in the 112th Congress.

[31] 3 U.S.C. 15.

[32] 3 U.S.C. 17.

[33] For further information on proceedings at joint electoral vote counting sessions of Congress, please consult CRS Report RL32717, Counting Electoral Votes: An Overview of Procedures at the Joint Session, Including Objections by Members of Congress, by Jack Maskell and Elizabeth Rybicki.

[34] For the proceedings at the joint count session of January 6, 2005, please consult Congressional Record, volume 151, part 1, January 6, 2005, pp. 157-173, 197-243.

[35] For further information, see CRS Report R40504, Contingent Election of the President and Vice President by Congress: Perspectives and Contemporary Analysis, by Thomas H. Neale.

[36] Paul Farhi, "Elephants Are Red, Donkeys Are Blue, Colors Are Sweet, So States Have Their Hue," Washington Post, November 2, 2004, p. C1, available at: http://www.washingtonpost.com/wp-dyn/articles/A17079-2004Nov1.html.

[37] Ibid.

[38] In the visible spectrum, purple falls between red and blue, and is often considered a blend of the two.

[39] Michael Barone, "States Aren't Red or Blue Forever," The American (American Enterprise Institute), March 13, 2012, available at http://www.american.com/archive/2012/ march/ states-arent-red-or-blue-forever.

[40] Ibid.

[41] A wide range of news organizations monitor and report on trends in battleground and other states during the presidential election. For example, see "2012 Swing States," Politico," at http://www.politico.com/2012-election/ swing-state/; or "The Electoral Map: Building a Path to Victory," New York Times, at http://elections.nytimes.com/ 2012/electoral-map.

[42] "Pundits Already Say Only 7-14 States Will Matter in 2012," National Popular Vote web site, available at: http://www.nationalpopularvote.com/pages/misc/hl_20110514_7-14-states-matter-2012.php. For further information on the National Popular Vote plan, see in this report under "Reform Through State or Non-Governmental Alternatives."

[43] Brendan J. Doherty, The Rise of the President's Permanent Campaign (Lawrence, KS: University of Kansas Press, 2012), pp. 113-114.

[44] The one person, one vote principle was established by the U.S. Supreme Court in congressional and state legislative reapportionment and redistricting cases in order to insure equal representation for equal numbers of people. See, e.g., Reynolds v. Sims, 377 U.S. 533, 568 (1964) and Wesberry v. Sanders, 376 U.S. 1, 7-18 (1964).

[45] Computed by CRS from "2008 Election Results," CQ 2008 Almanac (Washington: Congressional Quarterly, Inc., 2009) p. 10-8.

[46] Peirce and Longley, The People's President, pp. 119-127. Lawrence D. Longley and James D. Dana, Jr., The Biases of the Electoral College in the 1990s, 25 Polity 123-45 (1992).

[47] U.S. Congress, Senate, Committee on the Judiciary, Subcommittee on the Constitution, Direct Election of the President and Vice President of the United States, hearings on S.J.Res. 28, 96th Cong., 1st ess., March 27, 30 April 3, 9, 1979 (Washington: GPO, 1979), pp. 163-219. The validity of these assertions was, however, questioned by Peirce and Longley in The People's President. Writing of conditions in the 1970s, they maintained that the electoral college system actually disadvantaged African American voters. See The People's President, pp. 127-130.

[48] Some versions of the district plan would use ad hoc presidential election districts to award these votes, rather than congressional districts, but both Maine and Nebraska, which use the district system, tally their votes by congressional district.

[49] The District Plan became operative in Maine for the presidential election of 1972, and in Nebraska, for the election of 1992.

[50] Nebraska, Secretary of State, Official Results of Nebraska General Election, November 4, 2008, "Federal Offices: For President of the United States by Congressional District," pp. 10-11. Available at http://www.sos.ne.gov/elec/pdf/ 2008%20General%20Canvass% 20Book.pdf.

[51] U.S., Federal Election Commission, 2008 Official General Presidential Election Results, January 9, 2009. Available at http://www.fec.gov/pubrec/fe2008/2008presgeresults.pdf.

[52] Results computed by CRS. Data on District Plan electoral vote allocation for the 1992, 1996, 2000, and 2004 presidential elections are available to Members of Congress and congressional staff from the author of this report.

[53] Given that the strict proportional plan, by providing for fractions of electoral votes, would almost certainly require a U.S. constitutional amendment, and since the proposed Colorado constitutional amendment proposed a rounded proportional system, this method of allocating of electoral votes has not been included in this illustration.

[54] U.S., Federal Election Commission, 2008 Official General Presidential Election Results, January 9, 2009. Available at http://www.fec.gov/pubrec/fe2008/2008presgeresults.pdf.

[55] Results computed by CRS. Data on Proportional Plan electoral vote allocation for the 1992, 1996, and 2000 presidential elections are available to Members of Congress and congressional staff from the author of this report.

[56] Briefly, the National Popular Vote initiative (NPV) is an interstate compact or agreement by which each participating state agrees to cast its electoral votes for the candidates winning the most popular votes nationwide, whether or not those candidates won the most popular votes within the state. NPV's constitutional authority rests on the Constitution's broad grant of authority over the appointment of electors to the states. NPV will not take effect unless or until states that dispose of a majority of electoral votes, 270 or more, have agreed to the compact. For additional information on the National Popular Vote Plan, please see CRS Report R42139, Contemporary Developments in Presidential Elections, by Kevin J. Coleman, R. Sam Garrett, and Thomas H. Neale.

[57] The only exceptions might occur under variations that call for election by Congress in the event of a tie, or if no candidate receives a requisite minimum of votes, e.g. 40%.

[58] In this case, the "people's choice" is defined as the candidate or candidates who won a majority or plurality of popular votes.

[59] For more detailed information on reform proposals, please consult CRS Report R42139, Contemporary Developments in Presidential Elections, by Kevin J. Coleman, R. Sam Garrett, and Thomas H. Neale.

[60] At the time of this writing, the following jurisdictions, in chronological order, have joined the National Popular Vote compact: Hawaii, 2008, 4 electoral votes; Illinois, 2008, 20 electoral votes; Maryland, 2008, 10 electoral votes; New Jersey, 2008, 14 electoral votes; Washington, 2009, 12 electoral votes; Massachusetts, 2010, 11 electoral votes; the District of Columbia, 2010, 3 electoral votes; Vermont, 2011, 3 electoral votes; California, 2011, 55 electoral votes.

INDEX

#

A

B

C

D

E

F

T

U

V

W

Y